NATIVE AMERICAN
ART OF THE
SOUTHWEST

LINDA B. EATON, Ph.D.

J.J. BRODY, Ph.D., CONSULTANT

PUBLICATIONS
INTERNATIONAL,
LTD.

LINDA B. EATON, PH.D., obtained her doctorate in anthropology from Brown University and specializes in American Indian art and ethnology. She has served as museum curator and coordinator of American Indian exhibitions at several prominent museums, including the Museum of Northern Arizona and the Museum of Man. She has lectured, taught, and written extensively on Indian arts and archaeology.

J. J. BRODY, PH.D., is a renowned scholar of American Indian art and is currently a Professor Emeritus at the Department of Art and Art History at the University of New Mexico. He was former director of the Maxwell Museum of Anthropology and has organized museum exhibits, written books, and is a research curator with the School of American Research and the Laboratory of Anthropology.

Louis Weber, C.E.O.
Publications International, Ltd.
7373 North Cicero Avenue
Lincolnwood, Illinois 60646

Permission is never granted for commercial purposes.

Manufactured in the U.S.A.

8 7 6 5 4 3 2 1

ISBN 1-56173-279-6

Library of Congress Catalog Card No. 92-64287

PUBLICATIONS INTERNATIONAL, LTD.

CONTENTS

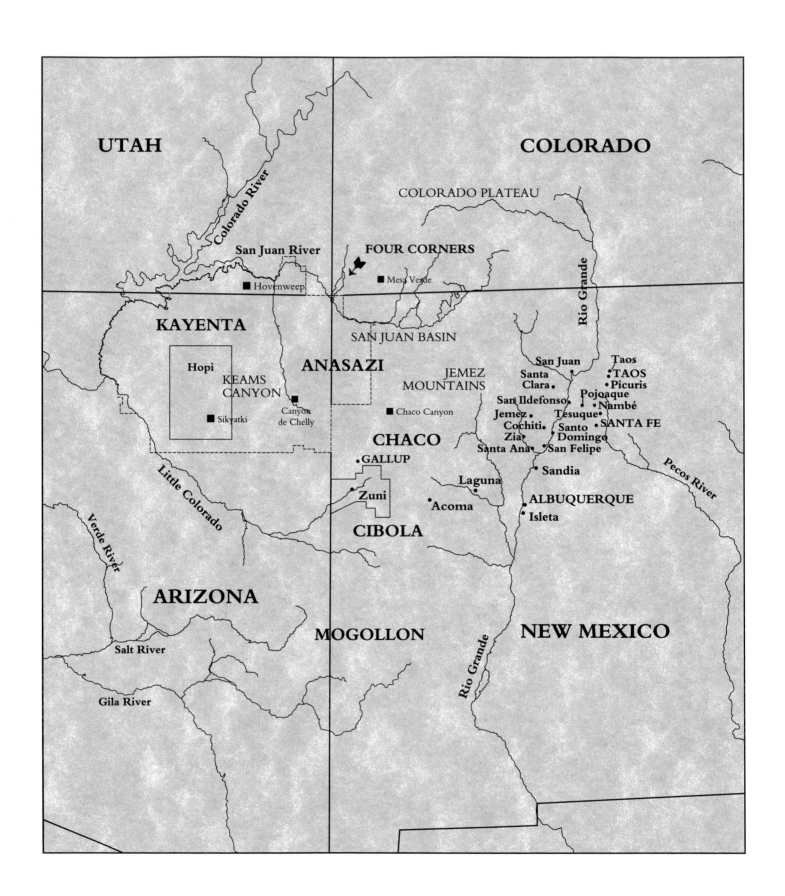

UTAH

COLORADO

COLORADO PLATEAU

Colorado River

San Juan River

FOUR CORNERS

■ Mesa Verde

■ Hovenweep

KAYENTA

SAN JUAN BASIN

Hopi

ANASAZI

JEMEZ MOUNTAINS

Rio Grande

San Juan

Taos

KEAMS CANYON

Santa Clara

• TAOS

• Picuris

Pojoaque

San Ildefonso

• Nambé

■ Sikyatki

Canyon de Chelly

■ Chaco Canyon

Jemez

Tesuque

Cochiti

Santo

• SANTA FE

Zia

Domingo

CHACO

Santa Ana

San Felipe

Little Colorado

• GALLUP

Sandia

Pecos River

• Zuni

Laguna

Verde River

• Acoma

ALBUQUERQUE

CIBOLA

• Isleta

ARIZONA

MOGOLLON

NEW MEXICO

Salt River

Rio Grande

Gila River

I

INTRODUCTION: A RICH AND VARIED HERITAGE

This map of the Four Corners area (where Utah, Colorado, Arizona, and New Mexico meet) shows the location of those villages known as the Eastern Pueblos as well as Zuni and Hopi, which are known as the Western Pueblos. The Navajo lands are located in northeastern Arizona and northwestern New Mexico.

A mong the native arts of the New World, few traditions remain as resilient and lively as those of the Navajo and Pueblo Indians. These Native American groups draw upon deep roots to produce art forms that reflect confidence in their way of life and to offer insightful responses to the changing world of the late twentieth century.

Native American Art of the Southwest focuses primarily on the Navajo people, the Hopi and Zuni of the Western Pueblos, and those groups called the Eastern Pueblos who are located along the middle and upper Rio Grande and its tributaries. Also included are the Acoma and Laguna groups who are located between the Western and Eastern Pueblos. All of these peoples have living art traditions practiced through a variety of media.

THE ROLE OF THE ARTS IN NATIVE AMERICAN CULTURE

Though widely appreciated and collected by non-Indians, the native arts of the Navajo and Pueblo Indians provide a key function within the cultures themselves. In all of these tribes, art occupies an important place in the economy. The appreciation by outside buyers keeps open a valuable choice for artists, which is the opportunity to make a living by doing work they love—

The Southwestern Association for Indian Affairs' famous Indian Market, held each August in Santa Fe's historic plaza, is a mecca for Southwestern Indian artists and collectors.

work that comes directly out of themselves and their heritage. Rather than conflicting with their traditional values, this type of work *supports* those values. It represents a viable alternative for artists who wish to remain in their homelands rather than seek wage work in the cities.

The arts play a vital role in maintaining these cultures as vibrant, independent societies, which ultimately contribute to the rich and varied texture of all of American life. Art allows Native Americans an important entrée into the cash economy while still maintaining the ideals and images of their cultures. Art also provides a way for Native American artists to articulate redefined ideals and values in a rapidly changing world.

Acoma is one of those villages or pueblos referred to collectively as the Eastern Pueblos. Acoma is actually located in New Mexico between the Western and Eastern Pueblos.

In addition to responding to changes within the cultures, Native American arts also react, at least indirectly, to the market for which they are intended. This large, non-Indian market has been very significant for more than a century. It has exerted pressure for both change and for an odd kind of conservatism in which the public's concept of "Indian" affects the Native Amer-

The marketing of Indian art in the Southwest provides a niche in which Native Americans can enter the cash economy by using ideas and techniques that relate to their cultural heritage.

Hanging in profusion on a trader's pegboard, these Navajo and Zuni concho belts indicate the artistry that has evolved since silversmithing was introduced to Southwestern Indian artists.

ican artist. Far from being "primitive" or static in conception, the work of these Native Americans is complex in design and refined in color, making use of many techniques and principles to express the artists' aims.

The Indian arts of the Southwest are perhaps more readily available than those of any other Native American art tradition. For adventurous buyers, reservation trading posts are still in operation, and opportunities to buy directly from the artists themselves are easily found in Southwestern cities, such as under the *portero* by Santa Fe's central plaza, or at any one of the large number of Indian art fairs. Southwestern Indian artists are even venturing out of their home regions as these fairs spread into other areas of the country. It is also possible to visit artists in their homes—a common practice for buying Pueblo pottery.

A large network of retail outlets also exists. Such outlets range from chic and formal galleries, where the work is usually carefully pedigreed, to roadside curio stands, where the work may or may not be Indian. In the case of the latter, some knowledge on the collector's part is required to find a genuine and satisfying piece. Not surprisingly, a vast import market of fakes and forgeries has emerged to satisfy persons fascinated with indigenous American arts. Also taking advantage of this interest are factory-style operations that employ Indians to produce work that is far from the one-of-a-kind, handmade pieces most collectors seek.

Although Navajo weaving is only about 300 years old, it is an art form that now represents this diverse and resilient people to most non-Navajos.

Within this welter, however, fine quality work exists. Although each group is known for certain specialties, primarily rugs among the Navajos and pottery among the Pueblos, a variety of media is represented in Southwest Native American art. For example, Zuni, Navajo, Hopi, and Santo Domingo jewelry has influenced the fashion scene. The basketry of Hopi is varied and spectacular, as is that found in the current Navajo/San Juan Paiute basketry revival. And, the carved animal fetishes of Zuni are a sculpture collector's dream in miniature.

Pablita Velarde painted "Kiva Mural—Symbolic Forms" in 1966. Velarde addressed supernatural themes in her work, which was unusual for a Pueblo woman. Daughter Helen Hardin also explored these forms and ideas during her career.

Southwestern Native American painting was traditionally a religious art, as in this fragment of a seventeenth-century kiva mural from the Hopi town of Awatovi.

GALLERY AND MUSEUM DISPLAY ART

While this book mainly explores arts that have long-standing traditions among these peoples, it is important to note that Western-style art schools have attracted Native American students. The Institute of American Indian Arts in Santa Fe in particular has been responsible for training many young artists in easel painting and modern sculpture as well as in other arts more commonly associated with Native Americans.

In the Pueblo world, the form of painting most like western European painting was mural art, which was used in religious contexts. Mural art was by no means the only form of painting by the Pueblos. A broad range of painting practices was

employed, from painting outdoors (rock art) to painting on textiles, pottery, and baskets (usually by women). Mural painting
was merely the closest in form to European painting traditions.
Given its use in religious contexts, mural art was
usually restricted to men only and not made for
sale. This, coupled with a great interest by collectors for paintings of esoteric religious ceremonies
(which were controversial for Native Americans to
depict), has affected the course of European-style
painting among the Pueblo peoples. For a few
generations, easel painting followed a unique path
away from the values of mainstream art, but a new
track developed in the mid-1960s that was more
compatible with the mainstream gallery scene.

Moving away from the depiction of ceremonial scenes for the curious and into the depiction
of artists' own visions, easel painting has carved out a territory
that is now less controversial in the artists' home villages and
more critically successful in the world of gallery and museum art.
The late Helen Hardin's haunting visions of ancient Pueblo
images, for example, seem more than a generation removed from
the more naturalistic Santa Clara scenes preferred by her mother,

*This fragment from a kiva mural is also
from the Hopi town of Awatovi. The
village was destroyed and abandoned at
the beginning of the eighteenth century.*

Pablita Velarde. At Hopi, great change is evident in looking at the late Fred Kabotie's work in comparison to that of his son Michael. At Zuni, where easel art remained controversial for a longer period, a new generation of painters work with images that range from Patrick Sanchez's lapidary-like mandalas to Duane Dishta's other-worldly visions of kachinas to Phil Hughte's delightful, often humorous views of life in the pueblo.

Navajo two-dimensional figural art is similarly rooted in a ceremonial past, that of drypaintings. These are highly formulaic pictures of the Holy People made of unsecured sands and pigments, which are destroyed after they have served their curative func-

"Trading Woman," a lithograph by R.C. Gorman, features the heavy, languid form of a Navajo woman for which he has become famous. Here she trades turquoise and shell jewelry and other objects of traditional native Southwestern life.

tion. Other important antecedents include Navajo rock art. Navajos who were introduced to Western conceptions of easel art soon adopted a new artistic track, which paralleled the ceremonial painting traditions. This new track involved painting genre and imaginative scenes. From early on, Navajo easel painting depicted scenes of everyday life, as can be found in the serene pastoral scenes of Beatian Yazz, or the energy-infused running

Navajo painter R.C. Gorman works from a model who is wearing the traditional Navajo hairstyle and dress. Gorman is one of relatively few Native American painters who has achieved recognition outside the Native American art community.

horses of Andy Tsinnijinnie. Among the current generation of talented artists, R.C. Gorman is perhaps the best known, while other fine painters, including Mary Morez, Michelle Tsosie Naranjo, Emmi Whitehorse, Grey Cohoe, and Baje White-thorne work out of deep wellsprings of Navajo imagery in ways that are uniquely their own.

THE ROOTS OF SOUTHWEST NATIVE AMERICAN ART

The arts of the Southwestern Native American groups are part of traditions that span many centuries. Understanding the cultural heritage that influences the work of most Indian artists provides a fuller appreciation of the subtleties of craft and design in the various art forms.

Today's Southwestern Indian art is deeply rooted in the history and prehistory of its people. This pot by Evelyn Vigil is a revival of an earlier glazeware type done by her ancestors at Pecos Pueblo, now abandoned. Descendants live in Jemez Pueblo.

This Red Mesa black-on-white animal effigy pot from about 850-950 combines a degree of naturalism, as it seems to strain forward, with the geometric designs of more conventional vessels.

Using animal effigies for pot handles, as with the lizard on this Escavada black-on-white pitcher from c. 1000-1100, survives in modern Pueblo pottery.

The Rio Grande Pueblo Indians, the Hopi, and the Zuni descended from the prehistoric people that archaeologists call the Anasazi, who in turn came from the earlier Paleo-Indian and Archaic peoples. This lineage goes back at least 14,000 years in this particular area. (The terms "Pueblo" and "Anasazi" are used to distinguish between the historic and prehistoric periods. The historic period began in the mid-sixteenth century when the first Spanish invaders referred to the Indian villages as "pueblos.")

The remains of the Anasazi culture are concentrated in the Four Corners area of New Mexico, Colorado, Utah, and Arizona, where the remnants of their stone cities attract millions of visitors annually. In the archeological remains of the Anasazi, most of the characteristics that unify the Pueblo world today can be found: a corn, bean, and squash agriculture; masonry and adobe apartment-house structures with round or square underground ceremonial rooms; a religion based on ancestral spirits who return to the village in the persons of elaborately dressed dancers; ornately decorated, coil-built pottery; fine basketry and textile traditions; and an affinity for shell and stone beads, mosaics, and carved animal figurines.

In addition to the Anasazi, Pueblo ancestry probably included people from the Mogollon, an ancient culture located along the southern periphery of the Anasazi, that lived in villages of individual pithouses. The difference in dwelling structures aside, the Mogollon shared many similarities with the Anasazi. They are probably best known for the fine pottery that comes from the Mimbres valley. Mimbres pottery, highly prized by collectors, was commonly decorated with designs of humans and animals. Most of the black-and-white Mimbres bowls have been found in mortuary contexts and feature a hole punched through the bottoms, which was done after they were decorated and fired. For this reason, archaeologists maintain that the vessels had been ceremonially "killed" for interment with the dead.

Mimbres bowls often feature representations of people or animals combined with the large geometric designs usually found on prehistoric Southwestern pottery from that time.

The variety of pottery designs of the Anasazi are revealed through these sherds from pots broken long ago.

Anasazi art forms are the roots of modern Pueblo arts and crafts. The most well-preserved art form found at Anasazi archaeological sites is pottery because of the durability of ceramic. Older Anasazi pottery was done in black carbon-based or mineral-based paint on a white or red body. Later, polychromes (pieces with three or more colors) began to be used, which usually featured white, brown, and black pigments on orange, red, or yellow ware. Bold and geometric designs dominated; paintings of humans or animals on pots were rarely done in early Anasazi work. However, ceramic figurines were produced as were effigy pots, which are vessels made in the likeness of an animal or other natural figure. Representational painting—that is, painting that duplicates nature or forms found in nature—is most common in pre-Hopi Sikyatki polychrome vessels, which are yellowwares that some collectors of Pueblo pottery believe are among the finest examples of the art form ever made.

Other notable prehistoric Native American art forms include basketry, which in the Southwest goes back about 7,000 years. The oldest known basket fragments show the twining technique. By the Anasazi period, such techniques as plaiting, coiling, and wickerwork were used, often with very elaborate

Mesa Verde pottery vessels, from the northern rim of the Anasazi world, were decorated with carbon-based, often glossy paint, different from the mineral pigments used in the central and southern areas. This dipper dates back to about 1200-1300.

Commissioned by Bandelier National Monument, this turkey feather blanket was patterned after an ancient blanket fragment found there. Woven around warps of yucca or apocynum, the feather or rabbitskin strips made warm, fluffy robes in cold weather.

decoration. These designs may have been created by using materials dyed in various colors before weaving, painting the stitches directly after weaving, or applying thick layers of pigment over the completed basket. Baskets covered in beautiful mosaics made of turquoise, shells, and small rodent teeth have also been found. Prehistoric baskets range from fine miniatures to coarse granary baskets of large proportions.

Prehistoric textiles are similarly varied and beautiful. Examples of textiles usually survive only in fragments, but whole belts, ponchos, and blankets have been found, affording an opportunity to look closely at these forerunners of modern

All of the Southwestern archaeological cultures had sophisticated textile-weaving traditions. This cotton brocade fragment belongs to the Gila Phase of the Salado Culture from the Lower Ruin, Tonto National Monument. It dates from about the late 1200s to the early 1400s.

This early twentieth-century bowguard shows the interesting silverwork that is typical of Navajo jewelry.

Pueblo weaving. In addition, painted and patterned textiles were pictured in rock and mural painting, which provide another way to study prehistoric textiles.

A native type of cotton became common throughout the Southwest between A.D. 700 and 1100 and remained important in textile making throughout the Anasazi period. Prior to that other plants had been used to make coarser fabrics, while flax-like wild fibers had been used for very finely woven textiles. Weaving was highly developed, both with looms and with finger-weaving methods. A variety of difficult techniques were employed while elaborately painted designs decorated the work. Warm blankets were created by cutting long strips of rabbit hide complete with fur, or birdskin with down, to use as the "yarn" in weaving. Equally as interesting were the blankets made from yucca fibers wrapped with turkey feathers, which were both cozy and beautiful. The latter was often woven via a basketry technique known as twining.

Anasazi jewelry can best be understood by looking at some of the older forms of modern Pueblo jewelry. Included among the jewelry-making processes attributed to the Anasazi period is a type of mosaic, most often used with shells or wood as backing. This mosaic process was commonly employed to make gorgets

Pacific shell and a variety of stones were combined with turquoise and an occasional Atlantic shell in prehistoric Anasazi jewelry. Similarly ground beads are still made in some pueblos.

(ornamental collars), with the mosaic bits usually made of turquoise, shell, or a plaster-like material. These bits were then set with lac or a naturally occurring asphalt. Bracelets made of cut rounds from a type of clamshell have also been found, as well as beads made of shell, turquoise, or other stones that have been ground into a form that looks like modern heishi (beads made of shell). Also common in the Anasazi culture were small animal carvings featuring holes bored for stringing—the forerunners of the fetish necklaces made at Zuni today. Metals, however, were unknown as jewelry materials until well into the historic period.

In comparison to the Anasazi, the Navajo people entered the Southwest much later. Their oral tradition suggests that they came to this part of the world about 600 to 800 years ago, and the archaeological evidence supports that general time frame.

The making of elaborate jewelry from a great variety of materials fueled prehistoric trade that went far beyond the Southwest. This Hohokam pendant dates to about 700-1200.

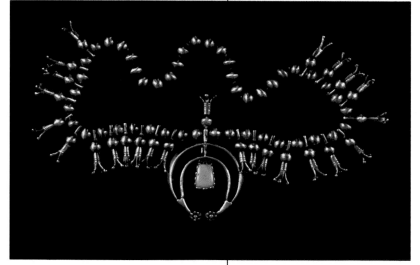

Above top: This necklace of nugget turquoise and Navajo silver beads combines the two materials for which Southwestern Indian jewelry is famous. Above bottom: A total of 47 globular beads and 24 pomegranate beads highlight this Navajo-made squash blossom necklace.

They probably came from the far north, perhaps central or northern Canada, where there are still groups who belong to the Athabaskan language-group to which the Navajo belong. When they arrived in the Southwest, they were probably still loosely connected to the people now called the Apache, though the split between the two groups came shortly thereafter.

Spanish colonists who followed Indian raiders back to their homes found that some of the groups practiced agriculture, though they moved periodically to follow game and wild plant resources. These forebears of the modern Navajo did not live in permanent dwellings year-round but instead built the forked-stick hogan still found in the most conservative parts of the reservation today.

Although Navajo prehistory is not well known, it is unlikely that the art we most associate with the Navajo people—fine weaving—was part of their lives prior to moving to the Southwest. However, they did make twined and flat-coiled baskets, and, probably late in prehistory, they developed a rough, dark, but well-made utility pottery.

Most authorities agree Navajo weaving evolved after contact with both Pueblo and Spanish colonial weavers. This supposition is partially based on the fact that the modern-day Navajo loom is very similar to the Pueblo loom. Scholars also know that Navajo women were highly prized as slaves in Spanish households because of their great skill with the Spanish looms. Whatever the exact derivation, Navajos probably learned to weave in the late seventeenth century.

Two hundred years later, silverworking technology was passed on to both Navajo and Pueblo artisans, making it one of the most recent Indian art forms. With that, the stage was set for the beginnings of Southwestern Native American arts as they are known today.

Present-day Indian crafts are thus living art forms, each with its own history and development. Whether it be basketry, which can traced back about 7,000 years, or pottery, which can be traced back about 1,500 years, or silverwork, which owes its existence to more recent influences, Native American art not only represents a rich past but is also a vital part of the future.

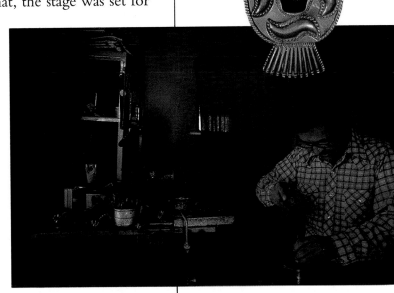

Above top: *Early concho belts, often made from Mexican coins, usually had round conchos and a diamond-shaped central cutout through which the leather could be seen.* Above bottom: *A Navajo silversmith plies his craft.*

II

THE EASTERN PUEBLOS

Of the native Southwestern tribes, the Eastern Pueblos—who still inhabit the valleys of the northern Rio Grande and its tributaries in New Mexico—were the hardest hit by Spanish colonization in the sixteenth century. Because their farmlands were among the most fertile and best watered in the region, their land became a magnet for Spanish settlement.

These groups were called "Pueblos" by the Spanish explorers because of their architecture—the multichambered houses

A glimpse of the ruins of the old church at Taos Pueblo can be seen behind the wall on the far left. One of the Eastern Pueblos, Taos is located just north of the city that bears the same name.

made of adobe and stone. Pueblo means "village dweller," which accurately describes the Pueblo lifestyle. Each Pueblo group was centered in a village, which functioned as an independent political entity. The Pueblos interacted through trade and occasionally through intermarriage.

Many of the pueblos that dotted the valley when Spanish explorer Francisco Vazquez de Coronado first saw it in 1540 perished in the early years of European domination. Survivors of the remaining pueblos were subject to severe pressures, which drove

Rainclouds gather over Taos Pueblo, which retains the apartment-house style that has been typical of Pueblo architecture for more than a thousand years.

their religion underground and pulled them economically into the Spanish colonial sphere. As a result, the people of these pueblos have led a highly compartmentalized life for centuries. Many traditional practices of the Pueblos have been kept private, while the lifestyle that has been made visible to outsiders has been affected by the larger society surrounding them.

Acoma potter Maria Sanchez readies a new piece of clay to add to the owl effigy she is building at right. Traditional Pueblo pottery is basically coil construction.

In most of the Rio Grande pueblos—in particular those nearest Santa Fe, Albuquerque, and other early colonial centers—many traditional arts have been lost. At least, they are not produced for public sale. Shell and stone jewelry, for example, now comes almost exclusively from Santo Domingo Pueblo. Basketry is virtually gone, as is most textile weaving; even pottery does not survive at all pueblos.

Instead, these tribes have shown great flexibility and initiative in understanding and developing the non-Indian market for their arts. In the nineteenth and twentieth centuries, they learned how to express themselves in ways that were personally satisfying and traditionally based, yet were attractive to non-Indian collectors. This gave them a solid place within the larger economy.

■ POTTERY ■

Pottery has survived at many of the Rio Grande pueblos, often as the only major traditional art. Form and design vary from one pueblo to the next, with certain distinctive designs associated with particular pueblos. The best known Eastern Pueblo pottery is produced at Santa Clara and San Ildefonso, both near Santa Fe.

Traditionally, the aesthetics of Pueblo pottery have been directly related to its function as a socially useful art form. Process, form, and design were inseparable from utility and community, making for a unity of art and social function that defined traditional Pueblo pottery. With the production of pottery for sale to the tourist, curio, and other non-Indian markets—which flourished after the arrival of the railroad to the Southwest—that unity became less vital. Thus, modern art pottery is not exactly in the same tradition as historic Pueblo pottery. It is closely related, but it is a different art for a different purpose in a different world.

Some potters continue to use the same methods that were used in the prehistoric era. In general, the process of making pot-

Above top: *In this 1930s photo, Santa Clara potters display their work for tourists.* Above bottom: *The shape of this polished black storage jar is typical of late nineteenth- and early twentieth-century jars from San Ildefonso and Santa Clara.*

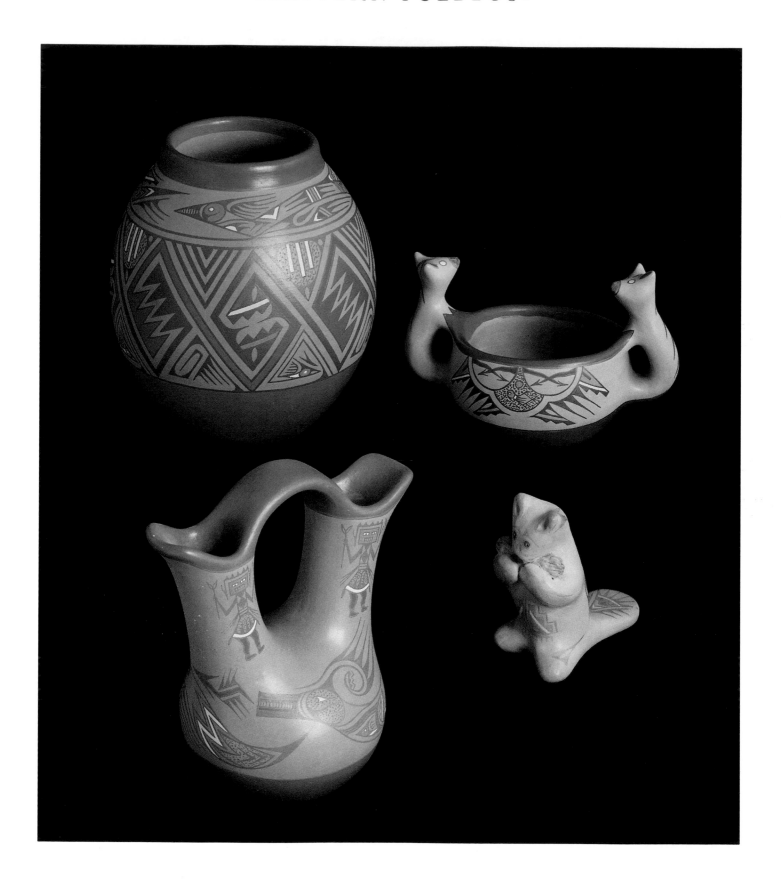

tery—from mining the clay to marketing the vessels—is a communal activity in which several family members and various generations take part. The social interactions involved, which at certain points are ritualistic, represent a meaningful part of the process. Raw clay is dug from local sources and then ground, refined, and mixed with a grit or temper. Most pottery is coil-built, meaning each piece is constructed through the building up of successive rolls of clay, which are pinched together and then scraped smooth to produce a continuous and unified surface. Most often, a clay slip (a thin, liquid clay) is applied or wiped onto the surface of the pot to provide a painting ground, like a canvas is primed in order to have a smooth, even background on which to paint an image. Polishing is done before firing, and the degree and style of polishing varies. Occasionally, slip is used as paint. Other types of surface decoration are done with mineral paints. Paint is usually applied with a brush made from a yucca leaf that has been chewed to make it soft; the brush then clings to the surface of the vessel and follows its contours. The vessel is then fired in a shallow pit using wood or dung.

Traditionally, Pueblo painted pottery consists of designs based on linear patterns within framed fields that are shaped to delineate the structure of the vessel. The fields are subdivided

Opposite: *The best known Eastern Pueblo pottery is produced at Santa Clara and San Ildefonso. These vessels were made by Margaret and Luther Gutierrez of Santa Clara, who are renowned for their whimsical animal figurines.*

Generally, a pot is dried, smoothed, slipped, polished, and then painted with designs before it is fired. Here Acoma potter Maria Sanchez paints designs on a vessel.

Although potters today take their wares to shows or to dealers to sell, much of their marketing is still done as it was 50 years ago, in their home villages to people who come to visit and to buy.

into smaller and smaller units. Most designs consist of simple, geometric figures, but complex symmetries involving those figures are often used. The interdependent relationship between the vessel's shape and design is representative of the Pueblo social community, with the vessel embodying the universe, the segmented design representing the Pueblo social organization, and the tiny, mutually dependent parts of that design representing individuals.

In general, the pottery of the Eastern Pueblos tends to be grouped by experts and collectors according to the language-family of the artists, reflecting age-old patterns of communication and interaction in the Pueblo world. The largest group is Tanoan, which is part of the Kiowa-Tanoan language family. Tanoan consists of three main languages—Tiwa, Tewa, and Towa. Santa Clara, San Ildefonso, San Juan, Tesuque, Nambe, and Pojoaque are Tewa-speaking pueblos, while the Taos, Picuris, Isleta, Sandia, and Ysleta del Sur Pueblos speak Tiwa. The only surviving Towa-speaking pueblo is the village of Jemez. Interspersed among the Tanoan speakers are the Keresans. The Zia, Santa Ana, Cochiti,

Santo Domingo, San Felipe, Acoma, and Laguna Pueblos speak the Keres language.

Contemporary Pueblo potters draw on an art form that is over 1,500 years old in the Southwest. They honor traditions and respect the history behind each vessel yet bring a personal touch to their work.

■ Tewa-Speaking Pueblos ■

Santa Clara and its sister Tewa-speaking Pueblos occupy the land directly to the north of Santa Fe. Its inhabitants have had regular and close contact with non–Indians for generations, and the railroad line built across Santa Clara lands in the late nineteenth century increased that contact, bringing tourists directly into the pueblo. The Santa Claras thus enjoyed an outside market for their artwork quite early and became the most prolific group of Pueblo potters.

They redefined their work as art for sale to outsiders at a critical time, one in which pottery could have easily died out. A new system of water wells had undermined the traditional need for certain pottery jars, resulting in the disappearance of certain types of Santa Clara ceramics. A nineteenth century white- or

Santa Clara potters Lela and Van Gutierrez made this polychrome vessel. Lela and Van are the parents of potters Margaret and Luther Gutierrez.

Contemporary pottery from Santa Clara, such as these pieces by Greg Garcia, retains the polished red and black surfaces used historically in the Tewa pueblos and popularized in the first half of the twentieth century for the tourist market.

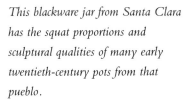

This blackware jar from Santa Clara has the squat proportions and sculptural qualities of many early twentieth-century pots from that pueblo.

cream-colored style of pot with polychrome decorations ceased to be made by the turn of the century, as did a red-on-tan type. A glittering style of pot made from mica-laden clay also became extremely rare, although occasional pieces are still made today.

With the change from ceramics as household items to ceramics as curios or *objets d'art*, two of the traditional pottery types of Santa Clara, a polished blackware and a polished redware, moved to the forefront. These two types date at least as far back as 1879, when examples of them were collected for the Smithsonian, but the increased importance of the outside market led to a series of design refinements in these pottery types. Additional responses to the new decorative function of pottery in general resulted in more changes. For example, the ability of pots to hold water became unimportant; many of the water jars made after 1930

would be damaged if water were actually poured into them.

Surface treatment and decorative techniques changed radically in the first decades of the twentieth century. In 1927 Santa Clara potters adopted a new technique for a highly polished blackware with a matte black decoration influenced by the pottery of San Ildefonso Pueblo. The clay turns black in the firing process because the pots are smothered in dung or sawdust during firing, causing a reducing atmosphere in which the carbon in the smoke is absorbed by the clay.

Carved designs appeared for the first time in the 1920s, probably inspired by the innovations of the great Sefarina Tafoya. The carved bands of animal designs on the shoulder of her pots, along with a fondness for fine redware polychromes, became lifelong hallmarks of her work. Her children, including the famous Margaret Tafoya, popularized this style of shoulder-carved pottery, which dominated Santa Clara in the 1940s. It was produced in both blackware and redware versions.

The deeply carved figures decorating the shoulders of pots are the descendants of earlier Santa Clara designs and practices. For example, nineteenth-century potters manipulated the clay by indenting the shoulders, making frilly edges, pocking vessel bod-

Above: *Teresita Naranjo made this deeply carved bowl, which shows the Avanyu, or plumed water serpent.* Below: *This type of large, polished black storage jar, made about 1941 by Sefarina Tafoya, is rarely seen today.*

Margaret Tafoya, shown here in 1985, is acknowledged as one of the finest Santa Clara potters of the twentieth century. Her work is much valued by collectors.

ies, and making dimpled bulges, among other practices. A prominent shoulder design was the bear paw motif, which was pressed into the vessel's body while the clay was still soft. The bear paw is a special Santa Clara design, honoring the bear who, it is told, led the Santa Claras to water during a long drought many generations ago. Another common design of the 1930s and 1940s was the rainbow band, in which the bands of clay placed where the neck of the jar joins the body deliver a prayer to keep the precious water inside from evaporating.

During the period from 1920 to 1970, new polychromes were developed on red, white, and buff backgrounds, usually painted with red, white, buff, and gray. Naturalistic figures and scenes began to be painted on redwares about 1940. A new sgraffito technique (in which a design is scratched onto a pot after it has been fired) was developed in the 1960s, which featured a buff-colored body visible through finely scratched designs in the polished blackware and redware. This type of pot remains immensely popular, with miniature versions especially prized.

Several new vessel forms entered the regimen or became common for the first time during the twentieth century. The most famous of these is the double-spouted wedding vase, a form since adopted by Indian groups across the United States for manufacture for the tourist market. There is some question as to the origin of this form. Some have claimed that it was introduced by a trader at the turn of the century, though earlier entrepreneurs

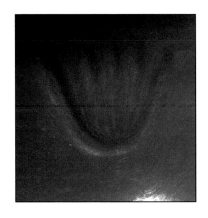

or traders may have innovated its use. A Santa Clara example in the collection gathered during an 1879 expedition organized by the Smithsonian shows that this form existed at least as far back as that date. It may have originated for use in Pueblo wedding ceremonies, which were the norm prior to the adoption of the Roman Catholic service, but the fact that none of the other Tewa villages traditionally used such a vessel suggests that, if this is so, the practice has no great antiquity. Whatever its age or original purpose, this form has become important in contemporary Santa Clara pottery and is widely sought by collectors.

In addition to the double-spouted wedding vase, a variety of other forms also developed, including vases, cups with handles, stirrup spouts, bird effigies, and waisted, "two-storied" water jars. Small clay figurines evolved as an important part of the tourist trade during this period, although they, too, date at least as far back as the 1879 Smithsonian expe-

Left and below: *A detail from this polished redware jar by Margaret Tafoya showcases the bear paw motif associated with Santa Clara. This motif is said to honor a bear who led the Santa Claras to water during a period of extreme drought.*

dition. Polished blackware "animalitos" by Manuel and Legoria Tafoya, who were members of Santa Clara's most illustrious family of potters, achieved great popularity about 1930. These little creatures, along with representations of Pueblo clowns and other human figures, persist to this day.

Other types of figural pottery produced at Santa Clara include the popular storyteller and nativity scenes associated with many Rio Grande Pueblo artisans. A storyteller scene consists of a large adult figure, usually depicted with his mouth open and eyes shut, with a cluster of small children sitting on or around him. Most recently, the large, pensive, and often humorous clay figures by sculptor Nora Naranjo-Morse have added to Santa Clara's legacy as a premier center for Pueblo pottery.

Perhaps the most famous artist in the history of the Pueblo world has been Maria Martinez of *San Ildefonso*, who often signed her work simply "Maria" or "Marie." She may have been the first Pueblo potter to sign her work. Maria and her husband, Julian, developed the polished black-on-blackware that made the potters at San Ildefonso famous and proved to be highly influential at Santa Clara Pueblo as well. Maria constructed the fine vessels, and, about 1919, Julian developed the

Nora Naranjo-Morse—from one of Santa Clara's most famous pottery-making families—has worked primarily in new forms, such as with this 33" figure called "Uncle Fidel's Cousin, San Luis."

method of painting black matte slip designs onto them. He may also have invented the use of powdered dung to create the reducing atmosphere that made the traditionally red San Ildefonso vessels black instead, although occasionally the Martinezes did produce their designs in redware. Maria and Julian worked together until his death in 1943, after which she worked with a variety of other relatives until about 1972. Maria died in 1980.

Before this black-on-black innovation, one type of San Ildefonso pottery popular with tourists was a polychrome consisting of black and red designs on a light-colored (gray, tan, or cream) background. This style, which was prevalent about 1880-1910, featured a flared neck that was sharply demarcated from the body. Often figures of birds and animals were rendered for decoration. This style was made by the Martinezes early in their career, before they popularized the black-on-blackware. Also produced at San Ildefonso was a black-on-red type of pottery, commonplace from about 1850 to 1930. By the 1920s, these types of pottery had allowed San Ildefonso to adopt an economy primarily based on the sale of arts and crafts.

Above top: *This 1935 photo shows the room blocks at one end of San Ildefonso's plaza. In the foreground is the entrance to one of the pueblo's two kivas.* Above bottom: *This San Ildefonso kiva jar was probably made in the early 1900s.*

Perhaps the most famous of all Pueblo potters, Maria Martinez of San Ildefonso, is shown here with her husband, Julian, about 1912.

This polychrome jar by Maria Martinez harks back to the old San Ildefonso polychrome, which was current when Maria learned her art. Although their black-on-black pottery was extremely popular, the Martinezes also made the older polychrome style.

A source of inspiration for San Ildefonso pottery styles and designs resulted from the archaeological expeditions of the early twentieth century. About 1909, Julian Martinez and other pottery painters began working as laborers at local archaeological camps while their wives did housekeeping and cooking at the camps. All became familiar with the fifteenth- to seventeenth-century pots made by their ancestors as well as the Mimbres tradition of the tenth to twelfth centuries. They were encouraged by the archaeologists to adapt the older styles and designs to their work, harkening a revival or renaissance of older styles.

A carved blackware style, in which designs are carved into the vessel before it is fired, was developed at San Ildefonso by the potter Rose Gonzales. Gonzales had married into the village from San

Juan Pueblo and began crafting pottery at San Ildefonso about 1929. Her work influenced later artists, who also worked with the carved and matte decorations, both in blackware and redware. In all of the styles, women customarily formed the pots while men added the decoration.

San Ildefonso remains a center for innovation in Pueblo pottery. The polychrome style that declined in manufacture in the early twentieth century was revived in the late 1950s by Maria Martinez's son, Popovi Da. He also generated a type of two-toned pottery that combined a polished red finish and a polished black finish. Both tones were generated by the same clay, but two firings were used to accomplish this effect. This style was later perfected by his son, Tony. Tony Da also specialized in

Left: *These polished black-on-black pieces by Julian and Maria Martinez are the type for which the couple are best remembered.* Below: *Maria Martinez in the mid-1970s, a few years before her death.*

Popovi Da, son of Maria Martinez, became a very well-known potter in his own right. In this 1968 photo, he displays some of the great range and variety of pottery he has produced.

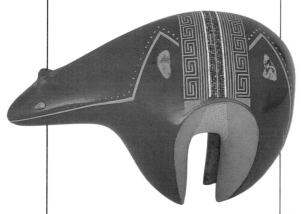

Tony Da, son of Popovi Da and grandson of Maria Martinez, continues the family tendency toward innovation. Tony Da's bear effigy in redware is inset with turquoise.

producing polished ware decorated with turquoise pieces or heishi.

Many contemporary potters, including several male artists, have developed distinctive styles based on traditional San Ildefonso principles. In addition to producing exquisitely graceful vessels, they have crafted elegant turtle and bear figurines. Sometimes these pieces have turquoise set in them or are adorned with elaborate sgraffito decoration. Smaller figurines, storyteller scenes, and nativity scenes are produced at San Ildefonso as well. Whatever the form, San Ildefonso potters create masterful pieces that exhibit great skill and artistry.

The largest of the Tewa communities, with a population of about 1,800, is *San Juan* Pueblo. San Juan currently specializes in polished redware pottery with incised geometric designs, such as cross-hatching and chevrons. The vessels are made of a micaceous clay, lending a slight glitter to the incised decoration. Recently, some potters have replaced the geometrics with figural and floral designs. Potters occasionally paint these incised areas and shapes in matte colors.

This pottery was probably based on late prehistoric northern Rio Grande graywares, which were also micaceous but not painted. Traditionally, San Juan redware, which dates to the seventeenth century, was left undecorated or decorated only with small lumps of clay. Only the upper part of the pot was polished.

Two nineteenth-century styles include a red-on-tan type and a polychrome in black and red on a white background. These styles, and the art of pottery making in general, nearly died out at San Juan. A ceramics revival around 1930 helped restore San Juan pottery making to its former importance. Two new types of polychrome have been introduced, one of muted matte slip colors and the other done in bright commercial paints. The new polychrome styles are clean and striking in their designs.

Prominent San Ildefonso potter Rose Gonzales, known for her carved decoration, made this pot about 1970.

Modern San Juan pottery tends to retain the old polished redware surface treatment but is now most often characterized by decorative incised bands.

Above: *This pot by Leonides Tapia of San Juan uses micaceous clays with incised and carved polychrome designs.* Below: *This vessel by Rosita de Herrera of San Juan combines the polychrome incising and carving with a traditional polished redware.*

Carved pottery forms are not commonly found in San Juan Pueblo, and, unless combined with incising, they are often difficult to distinguish from those of Santa Clara and San Ildefonso. Even more rare at San Juan are pottery figures, although a few storytellers have been produced.

Tesuque Pueblo, on the other hand, is probably best known for its "Rain God" figurines, curious pieces that were produced in large numbers in the late nineteenth and early twentieth centuries. They resembled pre-Columbian figurines in appearance. These forms had no religious significance and were distributed all over the United States from 1900 to 1940 in boxes of Gunther Candy. Since the 1930s, Tesuque rain gods have been decorated in brightly colored poster paints. Prior to that, they had been painted with traditional paints.

The little figures have generated much controversy—most of it unflattering—among scholars. Many scholars believe their features reflect the ideas white traders had about Indian culture more than any Tesuque ideals. However, a practice of making small figurines does exist at Tesuque. An 1878 Smithsonian collection from this pueblo contained small pottery figurines, and those pieces seem to have evolved, at least in part, from a long tradition of Pueblo Indian figurines that stretches well into prehistory. A few Tesuque potters have returned to this figural tradition, making storytellers, nativity sets, and small scenes from pueblo life.

In the eighteenth and nineteenth centuries, however, Tesuque was quite productive in terms of making pottery, furnishing household vessels to Spanish and Pueblo villages throughout the Rio Grande valley. The traditional pottery vessels made at Tesuque from about 1830 to 1910 featured elaborate black floral designs on a cream background. Interestingly, the bottom one-third of these vessels was covered with a red slip.

Early in this century, pottery sold to tourists became economically important at Tesuque. A black-on-red pottery type was produced for a short time around the turn of the century, but by the 1920s brilliant poster paints often replaced the more conservative natural pigments.

By 1935 the art was in decline, and very few Tesuque pots are made today. Of those produced, most common is a textured red-on-tan type that is reminiscent of a style made in the nineteenth and early twentieth centuries.

Tesuque "Rain Gods" were made at the turn of the century and packed inside boxes of Gunther Candy.

These two vessels are more typical of Tesuque pottery than the "Rain God" figurines for which the pueblo became known. The bowl on the left was made at the turn of the century, the jar on the right about 1890.

This Tatungue polychrome pot from Tesuque was produced about 1890.

The original pottery traditions at *Nambe* and *Pojoaque* virtually ceased before the present revival of pottery began at both pueblos. As at many Tewa-speaking pueblos, a polished blackware had been common during the historic period. At Nambe, it had replaced polychrome designs by about 1825. The surface of this Nambe blackware was distinctive in its slight sheen caused by the heavy mica concentration of the clay. At Pojoaque, a harder, less micaceous version of the blackware had also replaced an eighteenth-century polychrome.

Although pottery making was not an economically important enterprise at either pueblo throughout most of the twentieth century, a few blackware vessels were made until about 1950. At Nambe, some natural-colored micaceous pots were also produced, but the traditional styles eventually faded at both these small Tewa villages.

In recent years, a pottery revival at Nambe and Pojoaque has produced a great deal of high-quality ware. A textured matte polychrome pottery, a polished background polychrome, and polished red- and blackware are typical Nambe and Pojoaque styles. Pojoaque potters make a polychrome that uses pastel colors on tan, buff, cream, and polished red backgrounds, and they have also attempted to recreate the old eighteenth-century polychrome style. All pottery styles at Nambe and Pojoaque display a technical excellence and sense of imagination that is as well developed as those of other Tewa-speaking pueblos.

This Nambe jar, made by Lonnie Vigil in 1989, uses matte and polished reds, low shoulders, and a sparse design to make a striking, contemporary vessel.

Nambe-Pojoaque potter Virginia Gutierrez uses pastel polychromes and San Ildefonso/Santa Clara designs from a couple of generations ago to create a distinctive pottery of her own.

A graceful deer strolls around the shoulder of this turn-of-the-century Zia polychrome jar, which also shows the floral designs often seen on Keresan pottery.

The arcs of red ribbon delineate four separate Zia birds against a light gold or buff ground. This water jar dates to about 1910.

■ Keres-Speaking Pueblos ■

Some archaeologists believe the Keres-speaking groups descended from the people of the famous Anasazi sites at Chaco Canyon. Of these groups, the pottery of Acoma and Zia Pueblos is the best known.

The *Zia* have been great traders for generations, perhaps because their farmlands were so poor. One of their most important trade items was pottery. Puname Polychrome—a mineral-paint ware derived from an earlier glaze-painted pottery—was made from 1700 to 1760. It featured a brick-red body with a cream slip and was decorated in black mineral paint, most often in designs of feathers and arcs. A narrow band of red was placed around the rim and lower body.

Early Zia pottery features some unusual vessel forms. For example, the Puname jar's greatest width is located very low on the body while the bowl features a sharp bend just below the design field. From this shape evolved spherical jars with short, undecorated necks. This latter shape lasted from about 1760 to 1800. About 1780, the rim band was changed from red to black. Wide and narrow bands alternated in the main design field throughout this period, while red arcs became a common design element. These designs remained prominent in Zia pottery from about 1800 to 1850, though they did become bolder and less finely executed, while red banding was added at the bottom.

About 1850, however, this direction stabilized into what is now called Zia Polychrome, which remains a conservative but popular style to this day. Its naturalistic designs, including the Zia split-tailed bird, deer, and various floral motifs, play in and out of a wavy, sometimes double red line. Most of the designs are executed in black, but there are a few red elements and occasionally a pale gold color. The design background is a dull or grayish white, and often, the distinctive crushed black basalt temper shows through on this extremely hard-fired ware. Jar forms are high-shouldered; today, they occasionally feature a red-slipped base, which replaced the red band below the design field.

Contemporary potters also produce a few black-on-red-wares. In addition, some black or white vessels are made in which typical Zia imagery as well as less-traditional scenes involving dancers and eagles are depicted in acrylic paints.

Santa Ana Pueblo is located just to the south and east of Zia, and, as might be expected, Santa Ana pottery bore some resemblance to that of its neighbor. However, Santa Ana ware began to distinguish itself from Zia work about 1820. Although

This Zia jar from 1905 provides another version of the deer and the red-ribbon band that is sometimes used to frame designs on Keresan pottery. The hachured designs can be compared to the fine line work at Acoma.

In this large Zia polychrome storage jar from the 1900s, the typical Zia bird motif is repeated in the pot's two design bands. Here the Zia birds are separated by plant motifs.

Eudora Montoya, who kept Santa Ana pottery alive through the mid and late twentieth century, displays two of her creations, a jar and a large dough bowl.

The exact date of this Santa Ana polychrome jar is unknown. There has been relatively little pottery made at this pueblo in the last century.

it retained the mineral paints, brick-red clay, and feather and arc designs, Santa Ana pottery made use of unpainted crescent areas in the red band design, which showed the cream-colored body beneath. Santa Ana potters also tended to abandon the black edging that Zia artists typically painted at the juncture where the red and cream areas met. The surface was a rich tan until about 1880.

After 1880, Santa Ana pottery became almost white in color. Unfortunately, design execution faltered and pottery production decreased. By the 1940s, most of it had ceased. Pottery-making was preserved virtually single-handedly by Eudora Montoya, who became the backbone of a revival in the early 1970s. She and her students have preserved traditional techniques and designs, using old clay sources, sand temper, natural paints, and outdoor firing. Although the use of design is sparser than in the past, the new potters have resurrected old designs such as turkey eyes, clouds, lightning patterns, rainbows, and crosses. Current pottery from the revival features blocky red designs, broad lines, scallops, and distorted triangles. The Santa Ana revival not only produced pottery that was well received by collectors but it also preserved a part of that pueblo's tradition.

The pottery of *Cochiti* Pueblo from the historic period can be grouped into two major types. The Cochiti Polychrome, which is still produced today, is a very conservative style that can be traced back to 1830. It is distinguished by a light floral design in black and red on a gray surface. The Cochiti Polychrome also uses many figural representations in its designs, including clouds, rain, and lightning in addition to birds, animals, and humans. The clouds, rain, and lightning motifs were unusual for Pueblo pottery because they are considered sacred symbols. Cochiti potters regularly leave a spirit break in the black rimtops of their vessels. A spirit break is an intentional interruption in a design for ceremonial or religious reasons.

The other major type of pottery made in the historic period was the Kiua Polychrome, produced from about 1780 to 1920, though a few more recent examples also exist. The Kiua

Ivan Lewis of Cochiti Pueblo produced this figurine of a cowboy.

The appliquéd horned toad on the canteen to the right is typical of small Cochiti figures of the late nineteenth century. They were made free-standing or attached to vessels.

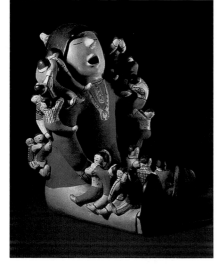

In the 1960s, Cochiti potter Helen Cordero began her storyteller figures based on memories of her grandfather telling stories to children. Storyteller figures are now made by numerous potters and at most of the pueblos.

Polychrome was also black and red on a gray surface, with the usual Keres red band under the design field. The designs, however, were geometric and bowl interiors were usually left undecorated. Occasionally, a row of dots crossed a bowl's surface. Like their Zia counterparts, Cochiti potters also changed the rimline from red to black in the late eighteenth century. The pots were tempered with grit and crushed quartz, which can often be felt on the pots' surfaces.

Contemporary Cochiti pots are typically black-on-gray or creamy white with brick red bases and interiors. Occasionally, a touch of red is used in the design. The main design field is a continuous, unbroken panel around the pot, framed only at the top and bottom. Design elements tend to be visually isolated, with no real attempt to make them relate to one another.

Cochiti potters have produced many figurines of people and animals since the turn of the century, as well as various types of effigy pottery. But today, Cochiti is best known as the home of the storyteller figures, which were originated in 1964 by the Cochiti potter Helen Cordero. Cordero also created nativity scenes, singing mothers, and a variety of characters from pueblo life. Her figures are done in cream-colored clay with black and red-brown painting. These are at least indirect descendants of a long-lived figural tradition at Cochiti Pueblo.

Santo Domingo is one of the largest pueblos of the Southwest, but its pottery production is not prolific. Pottery motifs at Santo Domingo have emphasized geometric designs, and these forms remain prominent. Even in the current Santo Domingo Polychrome, birds and flowers may be depicted but are often enclosed in a more traditional geometric shape. Although the present style is descended from Kiua Polychromes, as is Cochiti pottery, the main design field of Santo Domingo pottery is always paneled, giving the designs a more unified look.

This water jar features the black decoration on a cream slip band that is typical of early twentieth-century Santo Domingo pots. This style uses geometric motifs rather than designs based on models in nature.

In this pot, Robert Tenorio has reinterpreted the old Santo Domingo geometric design layout into a more squat version.

A recent water jar by Robert Tenorio combines the old Santo Domingo geometric style with a bird and flower from an alternative, less distinctive turn-of-the-century style.

The typical Santo Domingo pot of the late nineteenth and early twentieth centuries featured black-on-cream or buff arrangements of repeated black geometric shapes. The black rim-line contained a conspicuous spirit break. After 1900, birds and floral designs were used, and jars became taller with a flaring rim. Red design elements were extremely rare, though the red band at the bottom of the design field became an all-over red-slipped base after 1925.

An extremely conservative pueblo, Santo Domingo produces very traditional pottery for internal use, though it has responded to the outside market to some degree. In the early twentieth century, it produced many small pieces for the tourist curio trade. These pieces were often made with handles, but in general, they kept with Santo Domingo design canons. A few potters worked with poster paints for this outside market, and recently bright housepaints and commercial glazes have been used for these pieces.

As with their counterparts at San Felipe, Santa Ana, and Zia, Santo Domingo-born potters are prevented from making figurative pottery for sale by traditional religious beliefs. Storyteller figures made at Santo Domingo are by a Jemez woman who married into the village.

Only a few potters can be found at *San Felipe* Pueblo. That pueblo's decorated ceramic tradition was always slight, though utilitarian vessels were made. The little pottery that is currently made there is either black-on-gray or red-on-tan and represents cruder versions of types made at Cochiti and Santo Domingo. Although a few ceramic figures are made at San Felipe, they are made by Jemez women who married into the village, and they make use of Jemez clays and colors.

Very little pottery was made in the historic period at San Felipe. This undecorated bowl from about 1900 is red-slipped on both the interior and exterior and has extensive fireclouds.

Located well to the west of the Keresan heartland is *Acoma Pueblo*, reportedly the oldest continuously inhabited community in the Unites States. (Old Oraibi at Hopi, however, is sometimes touted as comparable in age to Acoma.) Acoma vessels feature some marked differences from the pottery styles of other Keresan pueblos, primarily because they are so dynamic. This is perhaps due to their continuing interactions with Zia and Zuni Pueblos.

In 1940, when this photo of Acoma's mesa was taken, the village on top was a hub of day-to-day activity. Many Acomas now live at the foot of the mesa, but the old village remains an important feature in their lives.

Historically, Acoma potters used a sherd-tempered, dark gray clay for their vessels, which were slipped white and decorated with a red rim. Jars were short-necked from about 1700 to 1760, with careful, fine designs. A lengthened neck came into fashion from 1760 to 1830, along with bolder designs and a volute (spiral design) of red edged in black, which was wrapped around the vessel's body. The rimline changed from red to black about this time, as it did in the rest of the Keres world.

Style relationships between Zia and Acoma pottery were very close in the second half of the nineteenth century, with the two sharing motifs, compositions, and structures. The most dom-

inant form in Acoma pottery was the water jar. The neck was decorated with a narrow band, while the body formed a large design area. Late in the nineteenth century, red-orange and black geometric and bird motifs were added to the Acoma design regimen. These designs persist to this day on the stark white field that typifies Acoma pottery. Design units were organized into complex interlocking patterns that covered most of the vessel, providing Acoma with one of its most common design systems.

Rooftops are important areas in Acoma life, as they are in most pueblos. Many activities are carried out there, and it is from the roofs that plaza ceremonies are observed.

Acoma potters have long created beautiful works for use among themselves and for sale. The large jar in the rear is from the early 1900s. Front left is a modern fine-line wedding vase, and at right is a Tularosa revival pitcher, inspired by a prehistoric type.

A recent Acoma pottery style is a fine-lined design, featuring adjoining hachured geometric shapes. This seed jar was made by Marie Z. Chino and painted by Vera Chino. The Chinos are well known for their pottery.

Lines were painted with utmost precision and design units were filled with black paint, red, yellow, or orange slip, and fine parallel-lined hatch strokes. Other pieces produced in the late 1800s included effigy vessels and small bird figures.

By the mid-1930s, other miniatures or figurines were commonly produced for the tourist market, including owls and turtles. Storyteller and nativity scenes have since been added to the figural types produced at Acoma. Some potters also combine vessels with appliquéd figures that appear to be crawling on or climbing out of the pots.

Some of the greatest innovations have happened within the past few decades. Particularly significant is the development of samumu—a pottery style marked by delicate, fine-line, hachured designs. Samumu designs are often combined with human and animal motifs borrowed from the ancient Mimbres. Lucy Lewis, head of one of the two most prominent pottery-making families at Acoma, may have introduced these ideas at the suggestion of Kenneth Chapman of the Museum of New Mexico. However, other equally reputable anthropologists as well as potters have also claimed credit for introducing Mimbres animals to Acoma pottery.

Above: *Lucy Lewis, one of the most famous and innovative of Acoma potters, is shown here in 1985.*
Left: *This Acoma olla, made by Lucy Lewis in 1963, features the floral-based designs, red-ribbon motif, and fork-tailed bird common on the pottery of Keresan-speaking pueblos.*

Acoma potters often take their inspiration from prehistoric pottery types. Here, Lillian Salvador has used lizard figures from the ancient Mimbres style for a contemporary bowl.

This 1985 Acoma olla, or water jar, by Lillian Salvador combines old Zuni and Acoma designs. Salvador's precise painting and careful finish-work emphasize the strength of the designs.

The relationship between Zia, Zuni, and Acoma has been close for centuries, with Acoma probably the point of interaction and transmission of design ideas. One of the Zuni designs adapted into the contemporary Acoma style was the heart-line deer motif. In this design, a line is drawn from the mouth of the deer to its torso, representing the path of its breath, which contains the animal's spiritual essence.

Prior to the 1930s, the design fields of certain Acoma vessels were uniformly filled with geometric and floral patterns. After this time, broad white areas became prominent on Acoma vessels, decorated with only one or two examples of one motif, such as a Mimbres turtle or a heart-line deer. After World War II, potters began to make extensive use of motifs from a local prehistoric ware known as Tularosa black-on-white. Thus, greater emphasis was placed on designs based on prehistoric pottery or designs based on well-established Acoma motifs, such as birds, flowers, and rainbow arcs.

Contemporary Acoma pottery typically features carefully executed geometric designs in black on white, or designs from nature in a polychrome that consists of black and red on white. Pottery bases are sometimes slipped in a red-orange. Also, a few white-on-black pottery types are found as well as some white corrugated vessels. Acoma pottery is known for its thin walls and light weight; some vessels are so thin and hard that they ring like bells when tapped.

Acoma Pueblo has been termed Sky City because it is located on a beautiful mesa. However, few inhabitants reside there full time. Acoma's tradition of excellently crafted pottery continues in the work of the potters who live in nearby communities or who reside in Acoma during the summer.

Laguna Pueblo is a small Keresan village that was established near Acoma after the Pueblo Revolt of 1680. Laguna borrowed virtually everything about pottery from Acoma. Thus Laguna pottery is a kaolin-slipped whiteware. It is decorated with black paint and with yellow, red, and brown oxide pigments. Red paint is frequently used to decorate the interior of both bowls and jars. Though not as well executed, Laguna designs are often similar to Acoma's, particularly the cross-hatching, geometric, and life-form designs. Solid elements in red, black, and yellow are especially common at Laguna.

Pottery at Laguna came to a virtual standstill after the 1930s. The art was preserved almost single-handedly by Evelyn Cheromiah until the 1970s. In 1973, a federal grant funded her efforts to teach a new generation of Laguna potters.

Contemporary Laguna potter M. Sarracino created this jar, which combines revival styles using Tularosa motifs with the texture of a corrugated finish.

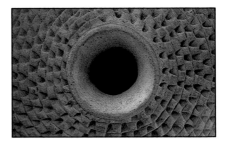

Among the prehistoric pottery styles that have been the subject of recent Acoma experimentation is the corrugated utility type from the eleventh century, as in this jar by Mary Ann Hampton.

■ Tiwa-Speaking Pueblos ■

These late twentieth-century Picuris pots show the light-colored, glittering micaceous clay used by that pueblo. The pot on the right is by Martinez; the one at left was made by Reycita Lopez.

Among the Tiwa-speaking pueblos, only *Taos* and *Picuris* have maintained any reputation for their ceramics. Historically, both of these pueblos produced a black-on-white carbon-paint ware, but this type of pottery disappeared about the time of the Pueblo Revolt of 1680. A decorated ware, it was replaced by a glistening gold or tan-colored micaceous ware similar to that of the Jicarilla Apaches, who were the neighbors and allies of these two pueblos during the revolt. These pots are most famous in a jar shape, which is prized in the Southwest as a vessel for making beans and chili. Handles, lids, and other useful features are common on Taos-Picuris pottery, but the vessels are usually undecorated or adorned only with punched or appliquéd designs. Fireclouds are also found providing beautiful serendipitous visual effects.

Designs at the two pueblos are quite similar, though Picuris vessels are generally lighter in color, harder-fired, and with thinner walls. Figurines are not commonly produced; those that are made are of the same micaceous clay used in the pots.

A paw print that crosses the boundary between a jar and its lid is another unique design by Taos potter Bernice Suazo-Naranjo. This vessel follows the Taos tradition of leaving pottery unpainted.

The pottery of *Isleta* has shown strong influences from a variety of sources, particularly in the twentieth century. This is not surprising considering the pueblo's lands are located in the urban Albuquerque area.

Isleta's earliest known pottery was a plain red-brown ware, but this was replaced with a black, white, and red polychrome by the beginning of the twentieth century. This type, which persisted until the 1940s, was the result of a strong influence from Laguna Pueblo or the influence of Laguna potters who had moved to Isleta.

In any case, this type of pottery was heavily affected by the curio market. Many pieces were small, simply painted bowls with twisted handles. Though made from a light red base, the body of the pot was decorated with geometric designs in black

Bernice Suazo-Naranjo has added contemporary twists to this lidded Taos pot with her use of the bear finial on top of the pot and a contrasting, red-slipped incised bear paw on the body.

Stella Teller, one of the leading figures in the Isleta pottery revival, often experiments with design and color in her work. A necklace of turquoise stones highlights this contemporary jar.

This Isleta polychrome pot from about 1915 features the white slip with black and red painted decoration characteristic of that pueblo.

and red on a white background. Laguna descendants now living at Isleta have recently revived this type, sometimes with glazed interiors for culinary use.

In the 1950s, poster paints were used to decorate pots, and recently, other nontraditional methods have been used as well. For example, a commercial white slip pottery decorated in orange and dark brown is currently produced. Though nontraditional pottery dominates, some traditional forms have survived. In addition, a few Isleta potters produce storytellers and nativity scenes for sale to the tourist market.

Pottery at the small pueblos of *Sandia* and *Ysleta del Sur* has all but died out in recent years, though both had a few potters working up until the 1930s. Recently there has been a modest revival, with a few red and black on cream-colored vessels produced at both pueblos. Ysleta del Sur vessels are often marked "Tigua" on the base.

■ Towa-Speaking Pueblo ■

The only surviving Towa-speaking pueblo is the village of *Jemez*, situated north of Albuquerque. Modern Jemez pottery is a new beginning for an art form that virtually stopped after 1680. Ancient Jemez pottery was a black-on-white type, and modern Jemez work is nothing like it.

Jemez pottery survived through the centuries only through a few pieces produced by women from other pueblos who had married into Jemez. Any necessary pottery was purchased from Zia Pueblo, and this is still true for ceremonial pottery. In the 1940s, however, a Zia woman married into the pueblo and taught the art of pottery making to her Jemez family members. They became the first new Jemez potters, and other women of the pueblo learned the art as well.

At first, the new pottery was painted in the bright show-card colors that were popular on curio pieces at that time, but within a decade a style had developed that was similar to the traditional San Juan redwares. The poster painted pottery had almost disappeared by the 1980s, but a type that consisted of orange, white, and black acrylic paints on tan paste increased. Another type of pottery developed that featured brown paint on

After a long hiatus, Jemez pottery was revived in the twentieth century and has since taken a variety of directions. This pot by Mary Toya uses a design based on a famous seventeenth-century jar from Acoma or Zuni.

a tan slip, which sometimes included terra cotta and black designs, with occasional turquoise elements.

Natural earth pigments are used on some of the finest pottery, although most pottery at Jemez is kiln-fired. In particular, the Gachupin family has developed a style using natural black and orange painted corn and geometric designs on a buff-colored background.

During the years that the production of pottery vessels had deteriorated at Jemez, one ceramic tradition did survive. And, it remains vital today. That tradition involved the making of clay figures. Jemez is now famous for its storytellers, nativities, and other figural scenes, usually executed in a tan slip with dark brown (or red-brown) and black lines.

Also living at Jemez are the descendants of the last seventeen inhabitants of *Pecos* Pueblo, another Towa-speaking group who moved to Jemez in 1838. Potters from this group include Juanita Toledo and Evelyn Vigil, who have recently re-created a fifteenth- and sixteenth-century Pecos glazeware. This pottery type is a redware in which a dark brown glaze paint outlines the cream-colored design elements. It also includes a spirit break in

Jemez has been a major participant in the revival of Pueblo figurines, such as storytellers. These unpainted, unfired figures by Maxine Toya appear to be singing.

Laura Gachupin of Jemez created this carefully polished and elaborately painted modern polychrome on buff jar now located at the Museum of Northern Arizona.

the line around the rim. Still another type of contemporary Pecos pottery consists of a light orange body with black and orange designs. With the success enjoyed by various Jemez artists in recent years, more potters are now emerging.

Pueblo pottery has continuous aesthetic ties to the past, with certain forms and designs going back hundreds of years. Yet it is an art form that has evolved over time, adapting to the changes in Pueblo life. The Eastern Pueblos share a common heritage, but, as this brief survey suggests, the pottery of each pueblo developed certain unique features of ornamentation, form, and technique. Pueblo pottery offers an understanding of the people who produced it: It signifies that the Eastern Pueblos have a long cultural heritage but at the same time reveals important differences between the groups.

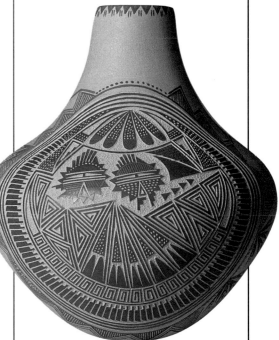

This modern Jemez pot by Glendora Daubs uses the sgraffito technique to delineate a contemporary version of a series of designs well known in Pueblo pottery.

■ JEWELRY ■

The mosaic work for which Keresans are justly famous was never supplanted by the introduction of silverworking technology. These Santo Domingo mosaic earrings of turquoise, coral, and white shell date back to the Great Depression.

Traditional Pueblo jewelry for thousands of years consisted of ground beads and pendants made of various stones and shells, rounds of glycimeris shell cut into bracelets, and colorful mosaics of these materials set in natural resins or asphalts on wood or shell backings. Although non-Indians tend to think all Southwestern jewelry consists of silver set with turquoise, the more traditional non-metal jewelry is what thrives in the Rio Grande pueblos today.

Turquoise was used in Pueblo jewelry long before it was combined with silver. The Keresan pueblos historically controlled access to the Cerrillos turquoise mines near Santa Fe, where pre-European workings have been documented. They mined the turquoise with stone hammers and picks made of antler. Rio Grande groups used other mines as far away as southern Colorado in pursuit of this precious, water-colored stone. Trade routes efficiently brought in shell, primarily from the Pacific but in small measure from the Atlantic as well.

By the late 1800s, only a small amount of cut turquoise was available, and the stone was recycled from old jewelry or imported by traders. By the 1920s, some turquoise mines were in oper-

The historical photograph at left shows an Isleta woman named Lupe Chiwiwi wearing a Cross of Lorraine necklace, similar to the necklace shown in the detail above.

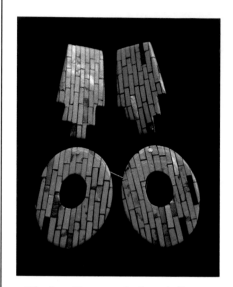

Charlotte Reano made these shell-backed earrings, which are inlaid with turquoise, abalone, and spiny oyster shell, in 1991.

These turquoise earrings, made by a Santo Domingo artist during the Depression, are mosaic, which is a jewelry technique that goes well back into prehistory among the Pueblos.

ation by private individuals, but none of the mines were owned by Indians. Today, Santo Domingo Pueblo is the major source for traditional jewelry made from turquoise and shells.

Perhaps most popular are strands of turquoise beads. These strands often feature beads interspersed with turquoise nuggets. Or, beads that are precisely uniform in size are strung by themselves on silky strands. Sometimes, turquoise beads are strung with beads of coral, pale orange melon shell, green serpentine, dark brown pin shell, or the light brown to white olivella shell, known as heishi. All of these latter bead types are also strung alone, as are beads from the deep purple spondylus (or spiny oyster shell), making for a wide variety of colors and textures. The beads are created by rolling and abrading. A truly fine set can contain beads that are quite uniform in size.

These beads also form the basis for the fetish necklaces of Zuni, in which the tiny figures of animals carved by the Zunis are interspersed with beads from the Rio Grande pueblos. A few fetish necklaces are entirely made at such pueblos as Santo Domingo and Cochiti. The animal figures on these necklaces are usually less detailed than their counterparts made at Zuni.

Mosaic work is also produced today, particularly at Santo Domingo. It most often consists of beautifully patterned work set on polished shell earrings, pendants, or bracelets.

The Rio Grande pueblos mastered silversmithing in the late nineteenth century, about the same time that it was learned by other Southwestern groups. Yet, silverworking has never attained great importance at these pueblos. Best known of the silver jewelry are the double-barred Lorraine or Caravaca crosses created early in this century. A specialty of Laguna and Isleta Pueblos, these crosses proved popular among Indian customers because of their coincidental resemblance to the dragonfly, which had traditional religious significance among the Pueblos. Currently among the Eastern Pueblos, a few smiths still work in silver.

■ OTHER ARTS ■

Among the Eastern Pueblos, with their ready access to larger American trade resources, few of the other traditional arts survive. Very little weaving is done among the Rio Grande pueblos, and basketry is virtually a lost art as well.

Basketry was primarily a male art at the Rio Grande Pueblos, which is unusual among Southwestern groups. Traditionally, a variety of manufacturing techniques existed, including plaiting. Plaiting—a technique using identically thin

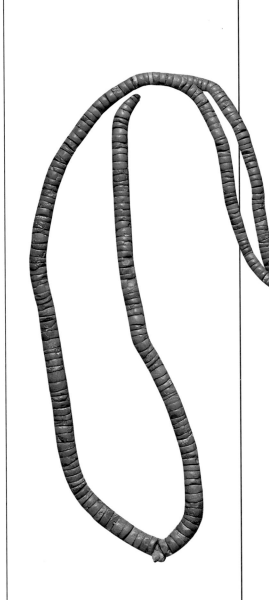

Santo Domingo Pueblo is the major source for traditional jewelry made from turquoise and shells. Most popular are strands of turquoise beads.

This thunderbird necklace by Clara Reano is an old Santo Domingo design that combines turquoise with white shell, jet, and coral. In some early twentieth-century versions of these necklaces, pieces of black phonograph records were substituted for the jet.

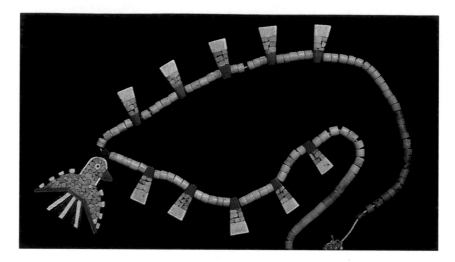

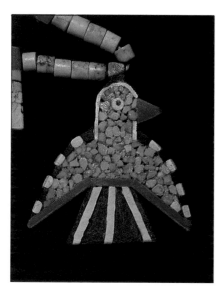

This detail of the thunderbird from Reano's necklace offers a closer view of the mosaic work.

and flat warps and wefts—survived into the modern period in most of the Eastern Pueblos and still exists today at Jemez. A round, shallow, bowl-like basket made of yucca, with a design of concentric diamonds or zigzags, was the most common type. (This style is similar to a Hopi yucca sifter though somewhat deeper.) An open-work wicker basket of willow has survived to the present, particularly at Santo Domingo, San Felipe, and Laguna. Wicker is a basketry technique that employs identically stiff horizontal and vertical weft elements. These baskets have straight, sloping sides, are solid at the bottom, and feature open-work around the scalloped top. The use of peeled and unpeeled willow withes allows some design play in brown and white.

Coiled baskets were also made in the Eastern Pueblos and survived through the 1950s at Zia and the 1960s at Jemez. New baskets from these groups are seldom seen today.

The weaving of cloth textiles was once a part of Eastern Pueblo life, but production has dwindled in the twentieth century to only a few belts and sashes. Currently, most traditional garments are either made of commercial cloth or purchased from Hopi weavers.

Items woven in the past included women's dresses—flat rectangles wrapped around the body and fastened on the right—and shawls or mantas. Also woven were breechcloths, fur or feather blankets, cotton or wool blankets, shirts with sleeves, belts and sashes, and various smaller items, sometimes knitted or crocheted.

The red and black medallions embroidered in wool on this shirt from Jemez consist of butterfly designs joined at mid-body. The shirt body, which is based on a prehistoric-style cut, is probably cotton and could have been made by modifying a Hopi manta.

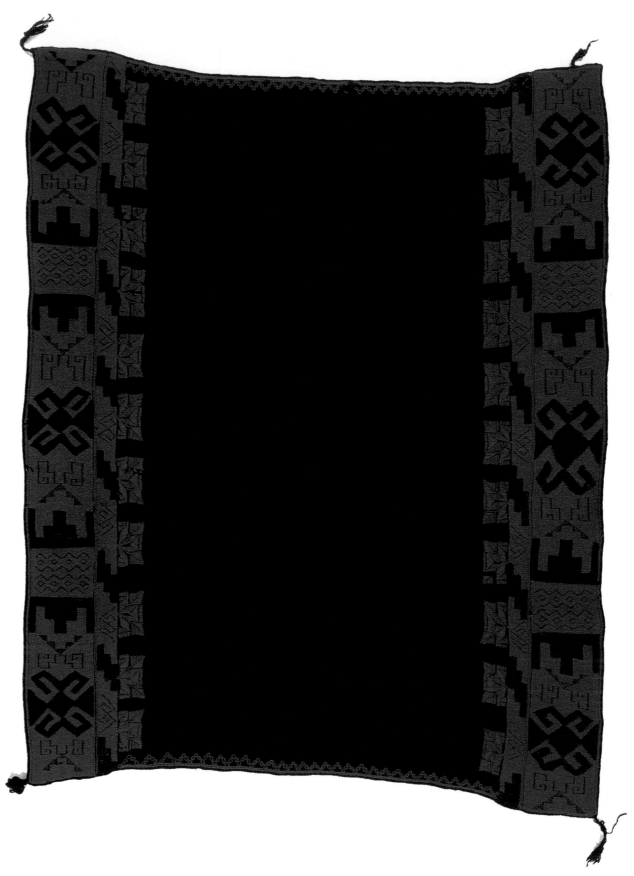

Most loom weaving ceased among the Tewa-speaking pueblos by or during the 1880s, although belt making has survived into this century. The people at Jemez grew cotton and made a number of textiles, a practice that continued into the twentieth century. In the past 50 years, however, they have produced only belts. Jemez is particularly known for its elaborate embroidered shirts. Among the Keresans, both weaving and the cultivation of native cotton persisted into the first half of this century at most of the pueblos.

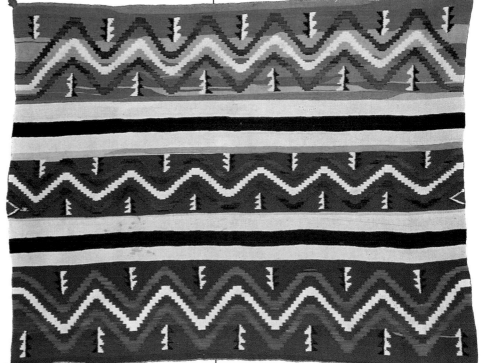

This unusual Jemez textile uses colors and designs to make a Pueblo version of what were called Eyedazzlers in the Navajo world.

Acoma Pueblo's textile industry was probably the most highly developed. With their embroidered wool and cotton shawls, the weavers of Acoma have produced the most intricately decorated pieces of the Eastern Puebloans.

The Eastern Pueblos have inhabited their lands for thousands of years, adhering to strong traditions of life and art. The art of the Pueblos is not only beautiful and innovative, it also encapsulates their history.

Opposite: An embroidered Acoma manta from about 1860-1870 illustrates the fine quality of their textiles and the distinctiveness of the designs of individual groups. Acoma mantas were perhaps the most elaborately embroidered.

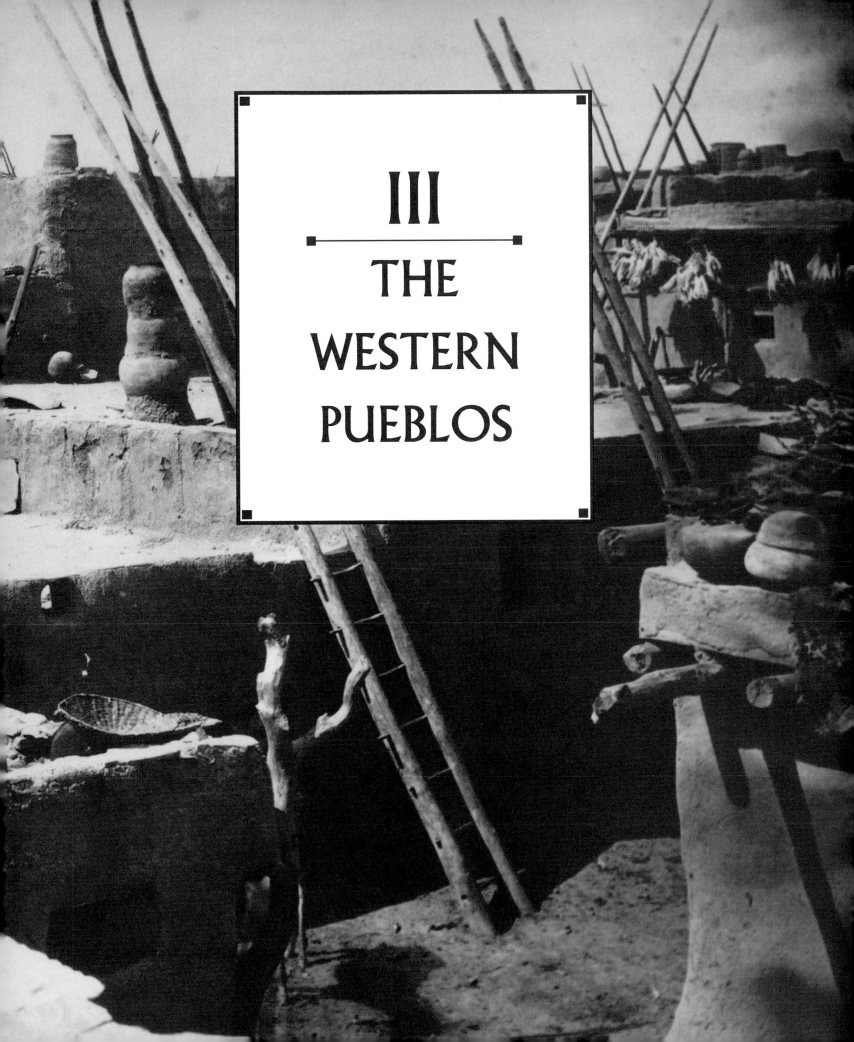

III

THE WESTERN PUEBLOS

ar from the Rio Grande, the people of the Hopi and
Zuni Pueblos farm lands where water for crops is
undependable and the entreaty of the gods for rain is a
constant and vital part of life.

Five hundred years ago, these uncertain conditions helped
make the lands of the Western Pueblos less attractive to the
Spanish colonists as well as to the later European settlers. This,
combined with other political and religious reasons, caused the
Rio Grande area to be colonized more vigorously. As a result,
the Hopi and Zuni remained more isolated than people of the
Eastern Pueblos, at least until the late nineteenth century. They
were able to continue more of their cultural traditions without
great interference, and such arts as carving, basketry, and textiles
survived uninterrupted at these pueblos. Access to these arts,

Though contemporary Zuni potters sometimes move designs from one framed band to another, it would have been unthinkable for the heart-line deer, rosette, birds, or spiraling rain bird motifs to appear outside the main "belly" design field at the time these pots were crafted in the early twentieth century.

Works by the Nahohai family are removed from a traditional dung firing. Here we see appliquéd turtles on the right and the plumed water serpent Kolowisi inside the cloud bowl at left.

whether through manufacture or trade, was and is critical to members of the Hopi and Zuni societies, because they are an integral part of the culture and religion.

▪ POTTERY ▪

Historically a woman's craft, Zuni pottery was prone to innovation. By the nineteenth century, several different types of pottery were produced at Zuni Pueblo, located in west central New Mexico.

These two Zuni pots from the beginning of the twentieth century illustrate two of the designs most frequently associated with the pottery of this pueblo. At left is the large rosette, which is of unknown origin, and at right is the deer with the "heart-line" connecting his breath to his heart.

The pottery of the Zuni people derives primarily from a whiteware tradition, though a crudely painted white-on-redware made a brief appearance in the late nineteenth century. The latter is now considered quite rare. Most pottery from the historic period consisted of black decorations in mineral paint, with occasional red and brown elements, on a white-slipped background. Zuni potters, especially after 1790, had begun to copy thirteenth-century and earlier Anasazi black-on-white pottery designs. This led to the nineteenth century renewal of fine-line hachuring, terraces, and rainbirds. Featherbird and butterfly designs from the eighteenth century were also incorporated as standard Zuni motifs.

Zuni potters were traditionally quite particular about the type of patterns or motifs depicted in the two framed bands that encircled various vessels. One of those bands was a wide field that stretched from the shoulder of the vessel to its rim; the other was located around the widest part of the vessel body. Some designs were reserved as neck decorations, while others were carefully relegated to the "belly" of the vessel. It is only in recent years that potters have become less strict about the specific placement of design elements.

As the nineteenth century passed, stylized plant, bird, and deer motifs were added to the Zuni design canon, along with repeated geometric patterns in black, red, and a range of browns. A large flower medallion, often called the sunflower or rosette, was a common body design, as was a spiral form derived from the rain bird. The rain bird is a parrot or macaw design that dates back to the early nineteenth century. On some pots, animals

This carefully painted turn-of-the-century Zuni pot shows the design canon appropriate for water jars of that time. The heart-line deer is a common Zuni motif.

were isolated in a small framed-off field, which is known as "the house" of that animal. Asymmetrical rectilinear and triangular designs filled in with diagonal cross-hatching or blocks of color were commonly used as well. In nineteenth-century pots, figurative designs dominated during the latter part of the century while geometric patterns typified the earlier years. Contemporary potters use both types of designs.

Perhaps the most distinctive Zuni motif was, and still is, the deer with a red heart-line leading from the mouth to the torso. This design probably originated about 1860. A motif featuring a small bird, which was equally as common, dates to about 1835. The sunflower and feather representations originated in the late nineteenth century.

Zuni potters also produced a very different type of vessel, which had its own set of designs. Called a cloud bowl, this vessel is a side-stepped, or terraced, bowl used for holding prayer meal. The terraces are stylized clouds and mimic the shape of Zuni altars. Cloud bowls often feature water-associated creatures, such as frogs, tadpoles, dragonflies, and plumed serpents. Also produced were fetish pots—jars that were supposed to be cages for fetishes. The latter actually seem to have been produced for collectors, with no authenticated use.

Above and below: *This prayer-meal bowl, made by Myra Eriacho in 1975, shows a number of sacred images, including dragonflies, a feathered serpent, and a heart-line bear. Such bowls are often kept in Zuni homes, and the prayer-meal is touched by family members for blessings during the day.*

This modern duck effigy pot by Priscilla Peynetsa was judged best of show in the Museum of Northern Arizona's second annual Zuni Artists Exhibition in 1988.

These contemporary pitchers by Randy Nahohai combine the heavy black outlines and hachured shapes that have been an important part of pottery design in the Zuni area for a thousand years. The balance and precision in the execution of the geometric shapes are a hallmark of Nahohai's work.

Effigy vessels have a long tradition in the Zuni area. Pottery owls, for example, have been made for the tourist market for more than a century. Other animals later joined the owl as effigy figures aimed at the tourist market, including ducks, serpents, lizards, and turtles. In addition, Zuni potters have long appliquéd clay lizards, snakes, and other creatures onto vessels, so that they appear to crawl on or into the pots.

Because the utilitarian functions of pottery declined at Zuni during the twentieth century, pottery making continued to decrease steadily. Many craftswomen took up jewelry making and silverwork instead, perhaps because these crafts paid better, their work is not as demanding, they have little breakage compared to pottery, and they are easier to market. But, Zuni pottery survived because important social uses existed for it that were divorced from the outside market.

In the early 1980s, a highly successful pottery revival began at Zuni, focusing on pottery for sale. As a result, the art is now flourishing in the village again. Historic motifs are being used to decorate the vessels, but the color palette has altered somewhat. A black-on-red pottery type as well as a red and brown-black on buffware have become more common than the traditional white-wares. And, both dung-fired and kiln-fired vessels are produced. Perhaps the best known potters associated with this revival are members of the Pcynetsa and Nahohai families.

Located in northeastern Arizona, the Hopi represent the westernmost group of Pueblo Indians. Two groups make up the Hopi, the original Hopi (many different clans, which seem to be descended from different groups) and the Hopi-Tewa. The latter are descendants of Tewa refugees who came to live at Hopi after the Pueblo Revolt of 1680. The Hopi-Tewa maintain a separate cultural and social order and retain a language that is distinctive. Both groups inhabit villages that are located on the First, Second, and Third Mesas, which the Hopi have occupied for hundreds of years.

The most characteristic Hopi pottery is a yellowware, though the amount of iron in the clay and the firing methods may cause the color to vary from yellow through shades of orange to almost red. A white-slipped type of pottery is produced as well. Most of the pottery is polychrome, though some simple black-on-yellow or black-on-red pieces also exist.

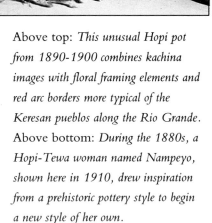

Above top: *This unusual Hopi pot from 1890-1900 combines kachina images with floral framing elements and red arc borders more typical of the Keresan pueblos along the Rio Grande.*
Above bottom: *During the 1880s, a Hopi-Tewa woman named Nampeyo, shown here in 1910, drew inspiration from a prehistoric pottery style to begin a new style of her own.*

Above top: *This Sikyatki revival pot is by Fannie Nampeyo, daughter of the famous potter.* Above bottom: *Nampeyo crafts a large Sikyatki revival jar in the wide, squat form typical of the style.*

Opposite: *Distinctive to ancient Hopi ceramics are the yellowwares. At top and left are Jeddito black-on-yellow pots and at right is a Sikyatki polychrome jar. Both styles are forerunners of modern Hopi pottery.*

The yellowware tradition extends back in time to the end of the thirteenth century, when the adoption of coal-firing began to produce an oxidizing atmosphere in the kiln. This led to the yellows and oranges now associated with Hopi ceramics. It also accounts for the most famous prehistoric Pueblo pottery style, Sikyatki polychrome. This type of pottery is characterized by a specific tendency in shape, which can be described as squat-looking or flattened. Its designs consisted of striking asymmetrical layouts, featuring an astonishing variety of life forms ranging from disembodied hands to kachinas to animals, birds, and insects. Also depicted were the phenomena of the sky, stars, rain clouds, and the sun. Sikyatki polychrome pottery emerged about A.D. 1450 and lasted until about A.D. 1600.

When American traders first came to the Hopi villages in the mid-nineteenth century, Hopi potters had abandoned the yellowwares and were making primarily a Zuni-influenced gray-white ware. Although such distinctive Sikyatki shapes as the flattened, wide-shouldered jar persisted, many of the design and color influences that had made Hopi pottery unique had disappeared.

Late in the nineteenth century, Nampeyo, a woman from the Hopi-Tewa village of Hano, stopped using the gray-white slip. Instead, she began polishing and painting the yellow clay

itself. Her husband worked on the archeological crew for the Fewkes Expedition of 1895 and brought her pot sherds of prehistoric pottery found at Sikyatki and Awatovi. Taking her inspiration from Sikyatki and earlier designs, she began what is now called the Sikyatki Revival. Other potters followed her lead. The new yellowware style is the foundation of the Hopi pottery market today.

Most Hopi pottery is made on First Mesa, the easternmost of the mesas. Pottery-making on Second and Third Mesas largely died out before 1900, with only few utility wares produced in this century. Very recently, a small pottery revival has occurred around Hopi's westernmost village of Moenkopi that consists of a kiln-fired polychrome on a buff background. Some painted pottery is produced at Third Mesa.

The primary pottery industry remains on First Mesa and centers around the descendants of Nampeyo and their neighbors. Many of the best potters are Hopi-Tewa. They concentrate their efforts on the careful painting of their Sikyatki-inspired designs, or other designs since developed, on well-crafted yellowware. They also specialize in the fine polishing of their vessels. Although some kiln firing does occur, dung firing is considered by most potters to be an important part of the process.

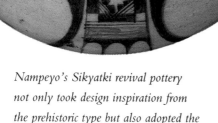

Nampeyo's Sikyatki revival pottery not only took design inspiration from the prehistoric type but also adopted the wide, squat jar forms of that earlier period.

◆ JEWELRY ◆

Jewelry making has become the art for which the Zuni people are best known. Zuni jewelry is remarkable for its exacting lapidary work and for settings that celebrate and enhance the stone or shell.

Although turquoise and coral are the stones most customarily set into Zuni jewelry, they also use a variety of other stones, including black jet (actually anthracite coal); pink, white, and yellow clam shells; abalone shell; spotted leopard and dark brown pin shell; green malachite; and serpentine (a green stone similar in makeup to turquoise), among other specialty stones. These stones may be set individually or combined together in figurative or nonfigurative designs.

The Zunis have also had a reputation for their fine stone and shell jewelry. They shared fame with the jewelry makers of Santo Domingo Pueblo as the best makers of stone and shell beads. Traditionally, this work has been sought after by other Southwestern Indians, particularly the Navajos. Many old necklaces worn by Navajos were in fact made by the Zunis.

The art of bead making survives in the form of the famous Zuni fetish necklaces. Today, the Zunis usually buy the spacing

Above top: *This fine concho belt reflects the Zuni tendency toward matching stones in size and color.* Above bottom: *This example of early Zuni inlay on a bowguard dates to about 1900-1925. It depicts a speckled frog surrounded by tadpoles, all inlaid into a red shell ground.*

beads from Santo Domingo or other Rio Grande sources but make the animal fetishes themselves. A variety of creatures are depicted in this miniaturized form: Birds are carved most often, but bears, frogs, owls, foxes, and mountain lions are among the animals also depicted. Sometimes the animals wear tiny "medicine bundles" of turquoise and shell on their backs. The carved stone or shell and the beads used as spacing vary as much as those used in other types of Zuni jewelry. Carvers make single- and multistrand versions of fetish necklaces, as well as very fine necklaces strung purely of fetishes with no spacing beads between them. Pete and Dinah Gaspar have won numerous awards with this latter style of necklace. Perhaps the most famous maker of fetish necklaces was Leekya Deyuse, who was active through the 1960s.

Most Zuni jewelry consists of fine stones set in silver, though gold is sometimes used today. In 1872, when the Zunis had been working in copper and brass for about forty years, a Zuni named Lanyade learned silversmithing from a Navajo acquaintance. Turquoise stones were added to the silverwork about 1890, and the two have dominated Zuni jewelry ever since.

This 1930s fetish necklace is by "Old Man" Leekya Deyuse, considered one of the finest of Zuni fetish carvers.

In addition to setting single stones and nuggets, three other techniques are used in Zuni silverwork. Clusterwork—a technique in which many carefully cut stones are placed in a single design—was being produced by the Zunis by the 1920s. Clusters of round stones, usually turquoise, were used first, but around World War II the first needlepoint was developed. In needlepoint, narrow stones that are pointed at each end are set into various designs, usually cluster-like patterns. Very tiny versions of clusterwork or needlepoint are called petitpoint.

Channel inlay, another type of lapidary work, began about the same time as clusterwork. In channel inlay, precisely cut shapes of stone or shell are set on or in a solid or hollow silver base, with thin strips of silver between each set. Each piece is completely surrounded by metal and becomes part of either a figurative or geometric design. A piece of channel jewelry usually contains pieces of all one type of stone or shell, but a variety of stones or shells may be used in a single example as well.

The third important type of stonework made at Zuni is inlay, which is sometimes called mosaic. Inlay probably dates back to about 1935, when silversmith Teddy Weahkee developed the technique after seeing prehistoric inlay from the ancient Zuni village of Hawikuh. In inlay, the tessarae (the stone or shell

This elaborate inlay piece shows Zuni skill and talent at depicting elaborate figures as well as their interest in religious themes. Depicted here is a Raindancer kachina.

This pendant illustrates true needlepoint, which uses tiny elongated stones in intricate, perfectly matched configurations.

A Hopi silversmith creates a piece of silver overlay jewelry. Hopi overlay consists of two sheets of silver soldered together—the design is cut out of the top piece and the exposed areas of the lower piece are darkened.

This belt buckle from the 1940s by Paul Saufkie is an early example of Hopi overlay, which was developed by Hopi artists working with Museum of Northern Arizona designers in 1939.

pieces) touch one another directly, rather than having silver bands between them. Inlay usually features several colors of stone and shell within one piece of jewelry and often depicts life-forms or supernatural figures.

Both men and women practice silversmithing and jewelry making at Zuni Pueblo, and their work is considered among the most highly prized.

The first Zuni silversmith, Lanyade, taught the art to a Hopi friend, Sikyatala, in 1898. At this early period, Hopi, Navajo, and Zuni silverwork were quite similar. Hopi silverwork did not have its own distinctive style until the late 1930s and 1940s. In the late 1930s, the Museum of Northern Arizona worked with Hopi artists to develop a type of jewelry that not only incorporated designs from older Hopi arts but also was visually different from other Southwestern Indian jewelry. The resulting jewelry technique was called overlay.

In overlay jewelry, a design is first cut out of a piece of silver. That first piece is then overlaid onto a second, solid sheet of silver. The area showing through the cut out space is blackened, emphasizing the design. This type of silverwork was slow to catch on with certain smiths, but in 1957 it was adopted as the official tribal style.

Early overlay pieces were highly polished, but by the 1960s a new technique was developed in which pieces were "brushed" with steel wool, giving them a soft sheen. The Hopis currently produce both styles. Although stones are occasionally added to the jewelry, Hopi overlay is primarily an art of silver or, more rarely, gold.

Today, Hopi overlay jewelry comes in a variety of designs, though the humpbacked flute player (on the bracelet and bolo tie) and the "man in a maze" (on the piece at the upper right) are common.

■CARVING■

In keeping with their tradition of fine lapidary work, the most prominent carving done at Zuni involves miniature stonework. Decorative fetishes, which are larger versions of the tiny animals carved for fetish necklaces, have become a major art form at Zuni in recent years. Like those carved for neck-laces, these tiny figures are connected to a tradition that reaches far back into prehistory. Large (real) fetishes have had sacred uses in the pueblo for countless generations.

To Southwest Native Americans, real fetishes are objects in which the spirits dwell. Traditionally, the most highly prized fetishes were those that required no carving at all, that is, stones that bore a natural resemblance to a particular animal. These were considered to hold the greatest power. A Zuni legend tells of a time when all animals were turned to stones by the gods. When they were finally restored to life, some of the animals were forgotten. In the creation of fetish-es for sale, however, there is no mystical power involved.

The carving on these decorative fetishes has become quite detailed. Many rival Japanese netsuke carvings in fineness and

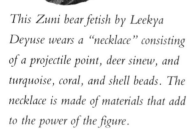

This Zuni bear fetish by Leekya Deyuse wears a "necklace" consisting of a projectile point, deer sinew, and turquoise, coral, and shell beads. The necklace is made of materials that add to the power of the figure.

beauty. Artists carve the fetishes from semi-precious stones and shells, as well as from more common rocks of the Southwest. They are as meticulously finished and polished as the stones in Zuni jewelry.

Originally, real fetishes represented the Zunis' beast gods of the six directions—the eagle, mole, bear, wolf, mountain lion, and badger, as well as such rain-associated creatures as the frog and turtle. The beast gods are part of Pueblo cosmology, which varies in detail from place to place. The people came up through three underworlds (evolving in each) to this earth surface (the fourth world), where each group then went in search of its "center place." In the early times, animals and humans could speak to each other, and human-animal transformations were common. The earth was divided into quarters along either of its two axes: North-South and East-West, or Northeast-Southwest and Northwest-Southeast. The axes cross at the center place, or earth navel, which is recognizable to each group by a special sign. The center place is also the point of access to zenith and nadir. It is marked in each village by the central plaza or a kiva. Each direction has its own attributes, color, and guardian animal. At Zuni, the beast gods are patrons of the hunt with healing powers. In the Zuni system, North is equated with the mountain lion and

This Salamopia (Warrior) kachina doll includes typical Zuni features, such as movable arms and the separately made clothing and ornaments. It was probably carved to teach children about the supernaturals. Zunis rarely carve kachina dolls for sale.

Right: *This Salako Mana kachina doll from the early 1900s represents a kachina from the Hopi version of the Zuni Shalako ceremony, borrowed from the Zunis in the nineteenth century. Below: This Hahai-i-wuhti kachina, the smiling mother-figure whose doll is given to new babies, has the fully articulated limbs associated with action kachina dolls.*

Opposite: *Hopi Kachina dolls symbolize hope of future abundance and are a way to teach children about the spiritual world. These two dolls date from about 1910 to 1930.*

the color yellow; West with the bear and the color blue; South with the badger and the color red; East with the wolf and the color white; Above with the eagle and with many-colors; and Below with the mole and the color black.

Today, however, decorative fetishes can represent other animals and figures, such as an African lion, a fanciful triceratops, a housefly, a dolphin, or almost any other creature a carver has seen or heard about. Occasionally a human or supernatural appears as well. Carried for luck or pleasure, or simply set on

Early Hopi kachina dolls, such as this Hemis doll from about 1895 to 1910, were frontal and visually static, which emphasized their immortal, and supernatural qualities.

shelves to be admired for their beauty, decorative fetishes are now widely collected by aficionados of Southwestern Indian art.

In addition to fetishes, kachina dolls are carved at Zuni, but priests of the Zuni kachina society object to their being made for sale. They have thus kept a very traditional form. They are usually blocky and made of a variety of materials added to the cottonwood doll. They usually wear cloth garments, feathers, fur, shells, and silver and turquoise jewelry. They are carved to teach Zuni children about the supernaturals.

At Hopi Pueblo, on the other hand, kachina dolls represent an important art form made for sale. The word "kachina" is used in three different ways. It refers to the supernatural beings of the spirit world, the male dancers who impersonate these beings in ceremonies, and the painted wooden figures that represent the dancers. The kachina spirits visit the Hopi villages to insure the continuing life cycle of all living things. They bring with them hope for renewal and rejuvenation. When the dancer takes on the likeness and the attributes of a kachina, he also adopts the role and the spirit he is about to play. A delicate relationship exists between dancer and kachina.

Kachina dolls, the most well-known form of kachinas, at least to non-Indians, are an offshoot of the much older custom of

carving small figures of the supernaturals for Hopi children, especially little girls. They are traditionally carved from the root of the cottonwood tree, because of the roots' tendency to reach toward water in this thirsty desert land. Kachina dolls are not only gifts symbolizing hope of future abundance but are also a way to teach the child about the Hopi spiritual world.

The oldest dolls were frontal and static-looking, sometimes with no articulated arms or legs. Only the head and body were distinguished as features. These types are echoed in the flat or cradle kachinas made today for infants. During the twentieth century, as collectors increasingly sought kachina dolls as curios or works of art, carvers began to make the dolls in active poses and color them with bright commercial paints. These types are perhaps best known through the work of Jimmy Kewanwytewa, who carved at the Museum of Northern Arizona for many years.

Carving has since grown more detailed and elaborate. Electric tools are often used in modern carving, though some artists still prefer finely honed case knives. Today the most skilled carvers can sculpt even the feathers and clothing out of wood in extremely naturalistic dolls, as typified by the work of Loren Phillips and Dennis Tewa, or in contemporary sculptures with kachina subjects, as done by John Fredericks and Wilmer Kaye.

Modern Zuni fetishes have become extremely elaborate carvings that are actually small sculptures. This landing eagle by Herbert Hustito is made of carved antler.

Loren Phillips works on an Ogress kachina doll in the contemporary all-wood style. Phillips's pieces are very naturalistic and are carved using a variety of modern tools and wood stains and paints.

Other, more conservative groups (such as the Zuni) choose not to commercialize kachina imagery.

■ BASKETRY ■

Although the Smithsonian collected a broad range of sizes, shapes, materials, and techniques of basketry at Zuni in 1879 and 1880, the art form is now extinct at this pueblo. Even as far back as the late nineteenth century, the Zunis were trading with other tribes to obtain many of their baskets. Traditionally, Zuni baskets were primarily of a coiled type, although Zuni wickerwork burden baskets and twined water jars can also be found in the Smithsonian collection.

The Hopi are really the only Puebloans who continue to make a full range of basketry. The Hopi women of Second Mesa are renowned for their fine coil basketry while those of Third Mesa are known for their wickerwork. Plaited yucca sifters are made at all of the Hopi villages.

Basketry survived at Hopi probably for some of the same reasons that pottery continued at Zuni in the absence of an outside market. Baskets have important social functions in Hopi life. They are necessary gifts at births and weddings. Once a family

Above top: *The life-giving kachinas are often depicted on Hopi baskets, as on this coiled plaque. Even in a difficult medium, the kachinas are given their essential characteristics.* Above bottom: *This rare Zuni basket is made of sumac and still retains some of its original vegetal-dyed design. Although production ceased in the early 1900s, Zunis still made a wide variety of basketry in the late 1800s.*

has received a basket as a gift, it is required that they return in kind with a "payback" basket. They are key parts of the women's basket dance and are given away by kachinas in some ceremonies. Also, Hopi wedding baskets (humorously called by the men "flying saucers") hang in a married couple's home. When the husband dies, the wedding basket carries his departed spirit to the traditional Hopi afterworld beneath the Grand Canyon. Although many of these baskets are sold to outsiders, their primary reason for existence is their place in the Hopi culture.

Hopi wicker baskets are made in a variety of forms. The wicker technique is the simplest form of twining, in which horizonal wefts are passed around vertical warps. In wicker, only one weft is used at a time, instead of the two that are used in regular twining. Perhaps the most common form of wicker basket is the flat plaque, a round tray basket traditionally used for carrying freshly ground cornmeal. Wicker plaques are extremely colorful and elaborate. They use any one of a number of traditional designs, all with Hopi names and

These three baskets illustrate the virtuosity that still exists among Hopi basket makers. The large coiled basket is by Martha Kooyestewa, the wicker plaque by Dora Tawahongva, and the small coiled bowl by Gertina Lomakema.

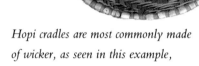

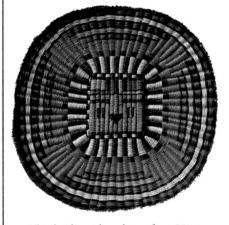

Hopi cradles are most commonly made of wicker, as seen in this example, which is stronger than plaiting.

This bright wicker plaque from Hopi was made with chemical dyes, though natural pigments are still made and used by some basket makers. The wicker technique is seen primarily on Third Mesa.

meanings. These same designs and colors are occasionally used for shallow "feather bowl" forms, and some have been adapted to deep bowl shapes as well. The dyes used to add color to the baskets were once all vegetal, but aniline colors are now replacing the old hues.

The wicker technique is also employed for other basket shapes as well, such as for the piki tray—a large, flat, rectangular basket with a plaited center, which holds rolls of Hopi paper bread. Another example is the deep, oblong peach basket that is strongly ribbed to support heavy loads. Hopi baby cradles are also made using the wicker technique. All of these forms are usually found in brown and white because of the natural colors of the outer and inner parts of the split sumac used in weaving them. Occasionally, cradles are colored.

Hopi coil baskets are made of shredded yucca fiber and use the natural off-white color of the yucca leaf as background. Green from the outer leaves of the plant is sometimes used as well, along with natural red-brown, black, and yellow dyes. In the coil technique, moving vertical fibers are sewn around stationary horizontal elements. Coil baskets can also be found in the shape of flat plaques or shallow bowls as well as deep-bowled or jar shapes. Designs differ from those used on wicker plaques, but they are equally as elaborate and varied and also deeply rooted in tradition.

The third, plaited type of basket is the utilitarian yucca sifter. In the plaiting technique, the horizontal and vertical elements are flat and thin. Both elements are active, crossing over and under each other. The yucca sifter—a flat, bowl-shaped basket made from the yucca plant—was originally based around a withe-rim, but current sifters most often use a metal rim for durability. Designs range from simple checkerboarding to various twill patterns. Sometimes two colors of yucca fiber, usually natural but occasionally dyed, are used to enrich the design.

The Hopi remain the greatest consumers of their own basketry, but they do make a certain amount for sale.

■ TEXTILES ■

The weaving of cloth textiles at Zuni now consists only of belt weaving, which is undergoing a revival at that pueblo. Kilts and other important flat weavings are usually obtained in trade from Hopi, whose textiles are quite similar to those made at Zuni in the past. In the past few years, however, one weaver has begun making kilts and mantas, doing traditional embroidery on

This old Zuni blanket combines a handspun, natural-colored background with bands of blue and brown Moqui stripes. Alternating orange and blue bands with green and white accents complete the design. The tan-gray color of the natural wool was typical of Zuni sheep at the end of the nineteenth century.

Hopi sashes are among the only Hopi textile types to have representational patterns. This sash design is said to show a Broadface kachina. The only design variation is the top-edge motif, which is the "signature" of the weaver.

A traditional Hopi-style belt pattern features a broad red band flanked by green and black stripes. The inner warp-float design may vary greatly, but the colors remain the same.

commercial cloth. Her work constitutes the first such garments produced at Zuni in about fifty years, and it remains to be seen whether or not these beautiful pieces will spark a rebirth in at least traditional embroidery techniques at Zuni.

In the past, weaving was done primarily by women at Zuni, unlike Hopi where weaving was a male art. Belts were usually woven on a backstrap loom; wider cloths were woven on an upright loom in plain, diagonal, and diamond weaves. Kilts, shirts, breechcloths, braided sashes, embroidered robes, striped and black wool blankets, and blue-embroidered, black women's dresses were the typical garments made. The main Zuni embroidery patterns were geometrics and stylized butterflies and flowers.

As with basketry, the Hopi textile weaving complex has survived fairly completely compared to that of other pueblos. Hopi men weave cloth both in their homes and in the kivas (ceremonial structures that are generally partially underground), and they maintain a broad range of types and styles. Until the past few decades, women wove robes that used rabbit fur wrapped around wool cord as the "yarn" for weaving. This custom has now disappeared.

The Hopis originally grew a native strain of cotton, though this practice ceased in the 1930s. Cotton was the basis of most of the Hopi weaving tradition, but wool was introduced to Hopi weavers when sheep were brought to the Southwest by Spanish colonists. Wool has traditionally been used to weave thick striped blankets and rugs, but these are becoming quite rare. In the past, wool was also used to make men's shirts in black-and-white checked or dark blue, but these are no longer seen either.

Commercial cotton is now used exclusively, and the cotton-weaving tradition remains very strong. This is probably because of the important roles handwoven cotton fabrics play in Hopi life. Traditionally, for example, a groom's family must provide a

This blanket is typical of the type that Hopi men wore in the nineteenth and early twentieth centuries as an everyday wrap. The stripes running the narrow width of the textile possibly indicate Spanish influence.

white cotton wedding robe for his bride, as well as a braided cotton wedding sash. Also, men's cotton kilts are an important part of kachina dress, as are traditional Hopi belts and sashes. These types of garments are sometimes traded to the Zunis and other Pueblo Indians for use in religious ceremonies, so they are also significant in the larger fabric of Southwestern Puebloan life.

Although no longer an everyday garment, the woman's dark dress is still woven at Hopi for ceremonial use. It, like the Eastern Pueblo garment, is a wraparound rectangle of black or dark brown, with borders of dark blue in diamond or diagonal twill weave. Heavy red and green yarns outline where the dark blue meets the black. Also woven but not used in daily life is a black-

A detail offers a better view of the Hopi wearing blanket of indigo blue with natural black and white wools.

Left: *This Hopi wearing blanket from about the 1850s combines indigo blue with natural black and white wools in the conservative stripes typical of early historic Pueblo weaving. Opposite: This Hopi woven manta dates to about 1910.*

black-and-white checked bachelor's blanket, which is sometimes called the little bird pattern.

Other items of clothing associated with Hopi weaving include the maiden's shawl, which is white with red and dark blue borders, and the wedding robe. The latter is a plain white garment, which is later embroidered in black and green at the top and bottom for further use. The wedding robe is very important, as it insures a wife's entry into the afterworld in the same way that a man's wedding basket serves as his "flying saucer." An elaborate white wedding or rain sash is braided by men also, with large balls of cornhusk covered by cotton yarn at the edges, and long tassels falling from these balls in imitation of rain.

All embroidery at Hopi is done by men. Natural dyes were once used almost exclusively, with indigo (for blue) and cochineal (for red) obtained from Mexico via trading. Aniline dyes are now increasingly common, and even acrylic yarns are sometimes used in embroidery.

Brocaded belts are woven on backstrap looms and are usually red with white and black used to create geometric, repeating

This embroidered Hopi wedding robe shows the style and patterns typical of Hopi embroidery on women's garments. The small, colorful insets in the black and green main pattern may contain any of a variety of natural and supernatural elements. The embroidery is usually added at some point after the wedding. In the ceremony, the robe is plain white.

Although collected as a Hopi saddle blanket, the relative complexity of the design and the closeness of the weave suggest that this textile probably originated as a wearing blanket of some type. The narrow yellow and brown-black "twisted" stripes lend interest to the design.

patterns. Sometimes green replaces black in these belts. Garters and head ties are woven in the same way.

In addition to the arts of pottery, jewelry, carving, basketry, and weaving, a number of small crafts used in Hopi life are sometimes sold and have thus become available to collectors. Small wicker cradles for dolls are produced, as well as a variety of traditional games and instruments. Miniature bows and arrows and brightly colored lightning sticks, which are given to young Hopi boys, are sold as well. A variety of gourd rattles have also caught the attention of collectors. Though often elaborately decorated to resemble various kachinas and other designs rooted in Hopi tradition, they are also adorned with other figures as diverse as Miss Piggy and Mickey Mouse—tongue-in-cheek reminders of the larger society that surrounds the Hopi mesas.

According to Hopi oral history, this type of robe was originally white with only broad indigo edge bands. As red became more readily available through European trade, that color assumed its present position and importance in the design.

IV

THE NAVAJO

This 1874 photograph of a Navajo named Ashtishkul shows the conservative stripes typical of textiles woven for Navajo use during that period. These simple designs survive today mainly in saddle blankets.

Perhaps the most important characteristic of the Navajo people that touches their arts is the flexibility and creativity with which they approach new ideas and new technologies. The Navajos were introduced to weaving through the Pueblo and Spanish peoples, while silversmithing techniques were acquired from their Mexican neighbors. But the Navajos quickly made these arts their own, creatively translating them into pieces that could be nothing but Navajo and adding exciting new forms to world art.

■ WEAVING ■

Navajo weaving probably developed in the seventeenth century, borrowed in part from Pueblo weavers and in part from Spanish colonial sources. Slaving by Spanish colonists was a common practice, and Navajos, who lived in isolated extended family units rather than thickly populated villages, were extremely vulnerable to slave traders. Spanish historical accounts mention the value of Navajo women in particular because of their quick mastery and great facility with the Spanish loom. A thorough understanding of the weaving process, though not the equipment, probably traveled with some Navajo slaves who were lucky enough to escape their oppressors. A knowledge of weaving was certainly in evidence when the Spanish were driven from New Mexico in the great Pueblo Revolt of 1680, a revolution in which many Navajos and Apaches played a part as well.

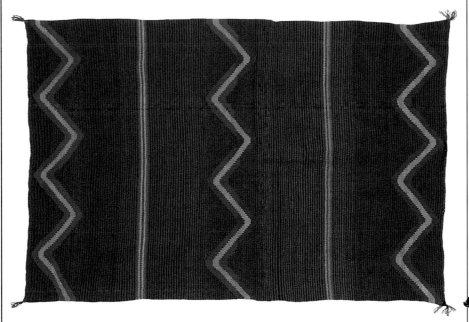

The indigo and brown-black Moqui (Hopi) stripes common in Classic Period textiles reflect the roots of Navajo weaving in Puebloan forms.

Following the Revolt, many apprehensive Pueblo Indians joined the Navajos in northern New Mexico, and the period from about 1680 to the 1750s saw a great deal of intermarriage and cultural and technological exchange. Many opportunities existed for Navajo women to see and learn Pueblo weaving processes at this time. Prior to this period of close contact, Navajos had been trading with the Pueblo people and had also raided them from time to time. Thus, they may have been exposed to the textiles and the weaving process even earlier.

Whatever the relative importance of the Spanish and Pueblo influences on Navajo weaving, there is no question that it quickly became a Navajo art. The Navajos were familiar with Pueblo basketry traditions, and designs from that canon, such as zigzags, equal-armed crosses, and terraced patterns, soon made their way into the Navajo weaving repertoire. The dignified banding

This 1870s woman's dress is made of two panels stitched at the sides and shoulders. The wide, black central strip and the elaborately decorated red bands at either end are typical of Navajo-woven traditional women's dresses.

This nineteenth-century Navajo dress, or bi'il, uses yarns raveled and respun from red flannel trade fabric. This was one of the earliest sources for commercially dyed yarns for Navajo weavers.

Opposite: The red yarns in this Classic Period serape (c. 1850-1860) are probably from raveled and respun trade fabric. The muted colors, the longer-than-wide form, and the design emphasizing the blanket's narrow dimension are typical of this type and period.

design from Pueblo blankets and the often frenetic diamond shapes from Spanish and Mexican traditions were adopted and reinterpreted by the Navajos, though the Yei (Holy People), and possibly the hour glass designs and bow shapes, were inspired by the Navajos' own world.

The earliest known Navajo textiles resembled Pueblo pieces of the time and made use of plain stripes, warp-float patterns, and twill weaves. In a twill weave, the weft threads are placed over two or more warp threads, with each series moved one strand to the right or left of the series beneath it. This process results in a diagonally ribbed effect. Throughout the eighteenth and early nineteenth centuries, Navajo weavers wove wider-than-long mantas (a shawl-like article of clothing) using natural

Woven of raveled, dyed bayeta and homespun indigo, ivory, and brown churro wools, this Chief Blanket uses a Third Phrase format but with much variation.

wool colors, indigo, and a few vegetal dyes, which were also known to their Pueblo counterparts. They also used raveled red yarns from commercial trade fabrics, such as bayeta. Bayeta is Spanish for baize, which was a closely woven woolen fabric napped to imitate felt. Originally from England, bayeta was brought to the New World in vast quantities.

The famous Patchwork Cloak, a well-known textile dating back to about 1804 or 1805, provides an interesting sampler of early Navajo weaving. It was made from 19 different existing weavings stitched together to form a new cloak for some lucky nineteenth-century Navajo. It includes patches from Pueblo-like

This rug from about 1890-1910, or perhaps later, makes use of the Chief Blanket design. In the Chief Blanket style, the full and partial diamonds are called points; the figures that center these diamonds are called whirling logs.

stripes and twills, and some fragments may have actually been taken from a Pueblo weaving. So similar were Navajo and Pueblo weavings during this period that the exact origins of all the fragments are difficult to determine.

By the 1820s, which begins the so-called *Classic Period,* Navajo blankets had become a highly sought-after trade item by Euroamericans as well as other Indians. Navajo textiles were considered better quality than pieces woven on European-style looms. As far away as the Plains, other tribes used and wore Navajo textiles. After 1850, more brightly colored commercial yarns became available, and patterns on Navajo blankets became increasingly more complex.

Navajos wove several styles of mantas during the Classic Period. Perhaps the best known is referred to as the Chief Blanket, which was a striped shoulder blanket widely traded among Indians of the day. Its design went through four phases in the nineteenth century, with each design more elaborate than the previous. The Chief Blanket has survived to the present, virtually the only wider-than-long Navajo weaving to do so. By the end of the Classic Period and into the Transition Period, Navajo textiles were invariably longer-than-wide, and they were vertical in their design compositions. The Spanish serape designs probably influenced the Navajo weavers in this direction. The serape style was based on Spanish/Mexican precedents instead of Pueblo types, and Navajo weavings of this style make for some of the finest textiles of this era.

This Navajo's blanket has bands of equal-armed crosses in stepped diamonds surrounded by eight-sided serrated figures. It is larger than usual for a wearing blanket, suggesting that it may have been a prop provided by the photographer or even a commercially woven bed blanket.

This bordered rug from about 1910, possibly earlier, combines cotton string warps and warm aniline-dye reds and golds with stripes and serrated and stepped designs.

When the American Southwest was ceded to the United States in 1848, the Navajos' nomadic lifestyle clashed frequently with that of the new American citizens, just as it had caused tension with the Pueblo and Spanish inhabitants before them. In the 1860s, many of the Navajos were displaced and rounded up. In March 1864, 8,000 Navajos were forced to walk to Fort Sumner at Bosque Redondo in east-central New Mexico, in what lives in infamy among them as "the Long Walk." At Bosque Redondo, which was 300 miles east of their homelands, they were interned. The internment affected Navajo life and culture on every level.

It was probably during this period that Navajo women abandoned the everyday use of their traditionally woven dresses for versions of the dresses they saw on the Euroamerican women around them. A style that consisted of full skirts and velveteen blouses had taken over by about 1890, which is a look that per-

This Third Phase Chief Blanket from about 1890 features pictorial elements of small weaving combs in two of its white stripes. The use of green in the serrated diamond points is also fairly unusual.

sists among traditional Navajo women today. Old-style handwoven dresses survive only as ceremonial garments. Also at Bosque Redondo, Navajo women were issued cotton string and commercial wool yarns for weaving to compensate in part for the loss of their sheep, most of which did not survive the grueling trip. A range of bright colors came with these new yarns.

The decision to move the Navajos to Bosque Redondo had disastrous results. The conditions there were deplorable: About one quarter of the Navajos perished, and the land was unsuitable for farming. The Navajos were allowed to return home in 1868, though the size of their homeland had been drastically reduced.

Navajo women took back to their homeland a new set of possibilities in terms of color and designs in their weavings. Right angle designs had typified the Classic Period, but during the Navajos' captivity, the army had provided them with a large

Woven wider than long, this Second Phase Chief Blanket still maintains great similarities to Pueblo designs. The blue in this early piece is probably vegetal indigo, while the red is probably from raveled yarns.

Woven about 1915, this rug makes use of the diamonds and broad stripes associated with the Third Phase Chief Blanket.

This Transitional Period weaving (c. 1890-1910) uses subtle Moqui stripes with a bright serrated pattern. The red section is woven from yarns made by raveling commercial cloth, then spinning the fibers for reuse.

Opposite: *Spider Woman is the supernatural who taught Navajos to weave. The dominant design in this Germantown serape is a variant of the Spider Woman's cross. Here opposed triangles replace the usually square "flags" on each corner of the cross.*

number of Hispanic blankets, featuring a different set of designs. Navajo weavers were heavily influenced by the Hispanic-based Saltillo style, characterized by a centralized pattern of serrated diamonds. The acute angles, dominant central design, and serrated diamond motif associated with that style were widely adopted by the Navajos during this period, though some Saltillo-styled blankets predate Bosque Redondo. By providing the materials for change, the experience at Bosque Redondo probably accelerated the design and color innovation that had already begun in Navajo weaving.

Between 1868 and about 1895, Navajo culture underwent a period of great change, now referred to as the *Transition Period*. Because the Navajos were allowed to return to only about ten percent of their former land base, the traditional economy was no longer viable. The federal government issued annuity goods to them, which included commercial wool yarns, commercial aniline and indigo dyes, cotton string, and commercial cloth—all of which contributed to new directions in weaving.

Traders settled on the reservation, providing a consistent link between the Navajo people and the larger market economy of the United States. Navajo products that could be sold for cash became an important part of the trader strategy, and the traders were particularly interested in increasing the outside market for Navajo weavings. During this period, Navajo textiles made the transition from blanket to rug. Many of the textiles from this period should actually be considered rug-blankets in that they

This textile (c. 1885) uses vibrant Germantown colors and the sharp serrations often found in Eyedazzler weavings. The design shows the color experimentation among Navajo weavers after they returned from the Long Walk and had access to bright commercial yarns and dyes.

This Germantown blanket (c. 1890s) uses zigzag and stepped patterns as well as the equal-armed cross, but here the weaver has arranged her design elements in an unusual pattern. The center stripe is a variant of the beaded stripe sewn on Plains Indian buffalo robes.

were woven by Navajos who thought of them as shoulder blankets rather than as rugs. Small saddle throws, which were decorative pieces used over saddles, were also produced. Usually quite colorful, saddle throws often featured busy designs with fringe and tassels in bright hues.

Weavers began experimenting with the bright colors of the Germantown yarns now made available to them. "Germantown" refers to a commercially spun, synthetic-dyed type of yarn, which had been named after the original town of manufacture—Germantown, Pennsylvania. These yarns were introduced by or came from trading posts. Also accounting for the wider range of colors during this period was the introduction of aniline dyes. These dyes, which had been invented in 1856, were introduced to the Southwest about 1880, probably by a trader named

This Eyedazzler was woven from bright Germantown yarns about 1880-1885. Eyedazzlers—among the most original designs ever created by Navajo weavers—were discouraged by traders in favor of bordered designs influenced by oriental rugs.

This close-up shows the sharply serrated zigzags and concentric diamonds that were common elements in Eyedazzlers.

Benjamin Hyatt at Fort Defiance. Aniline dyes were used to color handspun yarns.

With this wider color palette, the weavers created Eyedazzlers, aptly named for their use of brilliant colors and vibrant designs. A thin line of a contrasting color was often used to outline the major design motifs in the Eyedazzlers, making the colors stand out even further. These brilliant designs were apparently a Navajo innovation, responding to the new range of colors now available to them through Germantown fabrics and aniline dyes, rather than a style encouraged or developed by traders in response to the American market. In fact, in the early part of the twentieth century, Eyedazzlers were discouraged by traders.

Many of the rugs woven from the Germantown yarns were extremely finely woven. Cotton string warps were commonly

used during this period, a practice discouraged by traders at the end of the nineteenth century. At that time, most weavers returned to handspun wool warps.

One type of rug dating from the 1880s is known as the wedge weave, in which the wefts (the filling threads) were battened at an angle, forcing warps out of their normal vertical position and producing distinctive slanted stripes and scalloped edges. A lightning motif or zigzag pattern often resulted from this technique. Also developed in the Transition Period was the two-faced rug, in which a different pattern was created on either side of the textile. What was remarkable about the two-faced rug was that one side of the textile was woven out of the artist's sight. This difficult technique is still occasionally used today.

In the early 1890s, a number of traders encouraged the Navajos to stop using commercial yarns and return to the use of wool from Navajo sheep, and the Germantown fibers lost their prominence. By this time, few textiles were being made for Navajo use. Instead, rugs were produced primarily for the tourist trade or for shipping back to the eastern states.

Traders took advantage of the great interest in Indians that began growing back East, particularly the tourist market spawned by this fascination. They also attempted to influence Navajo

Don Lorenzo Hubbell of Hubbell's Trading Post kept small paintings of suggested rug designs to show to weavers. They were executed by Hubbell's painter friends back East and in California and were based on oriental rugs popular at the time.

Opposite: *In Eyedazzlers, sharp white or black outlined serrations literally "dazzle" the eyes, making it difficult for the viewer to focus on the textile.*

weavers to make changes in their own designs to suit Euro-american tastes. Perhaps most famous in this regard was Don Lorenzo Hubbell, who owned several trading posts from the early 1870s until sometime after 1900. His trading post at Ganado was probably the most influential in changing the course of Navajo weaving. Hubbell and other traders closely watched decorating fashions in the East. Hubbell actually collected small paintings of designs and colors that he thought would be salable in that market, which he showed to the weavers. He particularly favored red as a prominent color in rugs.

During the Transition Period, most of the motifs that became important parts of Navajo weaving were introduced. The Spider Woman's cross, an equal-armed cross with small square "flags" at the corners, proved popular in the 1870s and 1880s. Pictorial rugs, showing animals, cowboys, trains, and a

This Germantown rug from about 1890 features nine different rug designs in one textile. Of particular interest are two variants of the Tree of Life design, which is now, a century later, popular with collectors of modern rugs.

Hubbell's Trading Post is now a National Historic Site but remains a practicing trading post as well. Here Ailema Benally stands in the rug room of the post.

variety of other interesting subjects, became common at this time, as well as frets and hooks, arrows, feathers, and swastika-like symbols. These designs were first accomplished with the bright Germantown yarns and yarns from raveled commercial cloth, and then later with dyes on wool from Navajo sheep.

Designs and colors used on these textiles woven for out-siders were often bold and genuinely dazzling. At the same time, weaving for internal use had nearly ceased, confined to a few garments for ceremonial use and a steady market for simple striped saddle blankets, often of a thick, rough weave. The Navajo market for the latter continues to this day.

Finely delineated serrated diamonds create an exciting composition in this Germantown serape (c. 1885). Although serrated diamonds probably came from Rio Grande and Mexican Saltillo designs, they were quickly assimilated into Navajo patterns.

Though the quality of Transition Period textiles could be extremely high, as was often true of Germantown textiles, this was also the age of the "pound" blanket. Traders during the latter part of this period and early in the next often bought blankets and rugs by the pound. Weavers responded with thickly spun, loosely woven textiles. Stories survive about women who dampened or pounded sand into a piece to increase its weight.

From about 1895 to 1940, the weaving of rugs for the purpose of selling developed, driven largely by the traders and collectors' market. During this era, sometimes termed the *Early Rug Period,* the Germantown yarns fell into disfavor, just as the cotton string warps had done. Traders encouraged the use of rugs or blankets made from totally handspun wool. Many of the brightest colors, particularly green, purple, and orange, were discouraged, though red remained a popular and eminently salable color, as it is today.

Don Lorenzo Hubbell once again played a leading role in this development. He grew interested in Classic Period textiles and encouraged women to weave those designs and colors, producing revival textiles that were largely responsible for the survival of the Chief Blanket design and for a general range of colors. He standardized sizes and also took commissions for unusual sizes and shapes, including very large rugs.

Another influential trader was J. B. Moore, who owned the Crystal trading post from 1897 to 1911. He encouraged the use of certain design motifs that most white buyers perceived as

This rug from about 1920 is in the style known as Hubbell's Chief Blanket revival. The subtle dark stripes and the points are subordinate to the concentric serrated zigzags that were a minor part of earlier Chief Blanket designs.

Opposite: *A unique Germantown pictorial, this weaving from about 1890 shows a bird's-eye view of a mining operation. Two miners, an ore car, an ore bucket on a tram, a pick, a shovel, and a rake are illustrated.*

This Early Crystal shows the influence of J.B. Moore, who helped introduce oriental rug motifs to Navajos. The Anatolian design ("airplane" motifs on either side of the central diamond) is typical of Moore's Crystals.

Opposite: *With its elaborate borders and lozenge-shaped central elements, this rug combines the early Two Grey Hills style with cattle motifs.*

"Indian," such as arrows and swastikas. He also promoted the use of patterns associated with oriental rugs, which were popular at that time. The adoption of large, elongated central figures that stretched almost the length of the rug as well as the use of borders certainly resulted from the influence of oriental rugs. Rugs that had been inspired by Moore were usually woven in natural wools combined with an aniline red. Those of the best quality were made from commercially cleaned Navajo wool that had been dyed under the supervision of Moore's wife. These characteristics made up what is now called the Early Crystal rug.

The concept of a bordered textile was certainly not Navajo. In the words of one modern weaver, "Navajos always like to have a way out." So the idea of a closed border around a weaving was (and still is) disturbing to many traditional weavers. The popularity of bordered designs in the outside market was undeni-

Weavers of the Two Grey Hills area are traditionally fine practioners of their art. This tapestry is extremely finely spun and woven; its version of the Two Grey Hills design is intricate and carefully balanced.

This rug by Rose Mike is called a Two Grey Hills "tapestry" because of the extraordinary fineness of its spinning and weaving. This tapestry has 120 wefts per inch.

able, however. Moore and other traders began to reward weavers who used this layout, as well as the other designs and colors they wanted, by paying very well for these pieces. Not surprisingly, Navajo weavers looked for a way out of this quandary and found it in the "pathway" or "spirit passage," which is a small break in the border of the rug. Sometimes, it consists simply of one strand of yarn of a different color crossing the border. The pathway or spirit passage remains a common feature in bordered rugs to this day, particularly in pieces from extremely conservative areas of the reservation such as Two Grey Hills.

In many cases, regional styles were concentrated around certain trading posts. Often, rug styles took their names from those posts, which was the case with the styles known as Ganado and Two Grey Hills. These styles reflected, at least in part, the buying tastes of the local trader and the markets he supplied. They also exhibited the tastes, skills, and interests of the local

The Ganado style that developed around Hubbell's Trading Post combined rich reds, grays, and blacks with strong central lozenge-shaped designs.

weaving families. However, not *all* patterns could be assigned to specific areas.

Also, most weavers from the Early Rug Period did not strictly adhere to regional styles. Instead, they continued to experiment and produce original designs of interest to themselves. They trusted the market to find the right buyers for their one-of-a-kind textiles, which is still true today.

Several *Contemporary* styles reveal the visual power of Navajo weavings, particularly in the expressive use of color and the energy contained within the designs. Though the trader-influenced designs dominate, weavers continue to make innovations within these styles. The following listing of the best-known modern styles offers a general indication of the wide range of Navajo weaving.

Sarah Begay wove this contemporary prize-winning Ganado red rug. Its design is typical of modern Ganados.

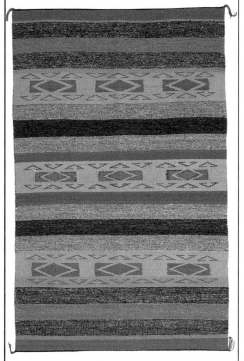

The modern, unbordered Crystal style uses warm vegetal tones in elaborate decorated bands alternating with plain stripes in natural or vegetal colors.

Opposite: *As indicated in this map of the Navajo territory, certain rug styles are associated with specific locations.*

The style called Chinle resulted from the efforts of a woman named Mary Cabot Wheelwright. In the 1920s and 1930s, Wheelwright, a member of the Eastern Association on Indian Affairs, became very interested in Navajo weaving. She tried to influence weavers to turn away from oriental-inspired designs and return to Navajo designs of the 1800s, particularly banded types. Wheelwright also supported a return to native vegetal dyes and the use of better quality commercial dyes. In hopes of accomplishing her purpose, she sent sketches and photos of traditional patterns to traders in the Chinle area, as well as to schools, weavers, and other traders. Unbordered styles cropped up at Chinle using a combination of vegetal dyes with a few chemical dyes, with some black in the patterns. Many Chinle types were woven in browns and golds, along with natural wools in whites and grays. Weavers often used a simplified version of the old serrated diamond motif. The Chinle style is in decline today.

The rug style now known as Crystal bears little relationship to the Early Crystal design. Instead, it is more closely akin to Wheelwright's ideals. Since the 1940s, the typical rug style from the Crystal vicinity has been banded and unbordered, with vegetal-dyed yarns in warm golds, browns, and greens. Crystal rugs are most frequently done in medium tones, but they are occasionally rendered in very pale or very dark palettes. Though a variety of patterns can be found in the bands of color, a common type is a two-color, wavy line pattern made by alternating two wefts of one color with two of another. The weavers of this

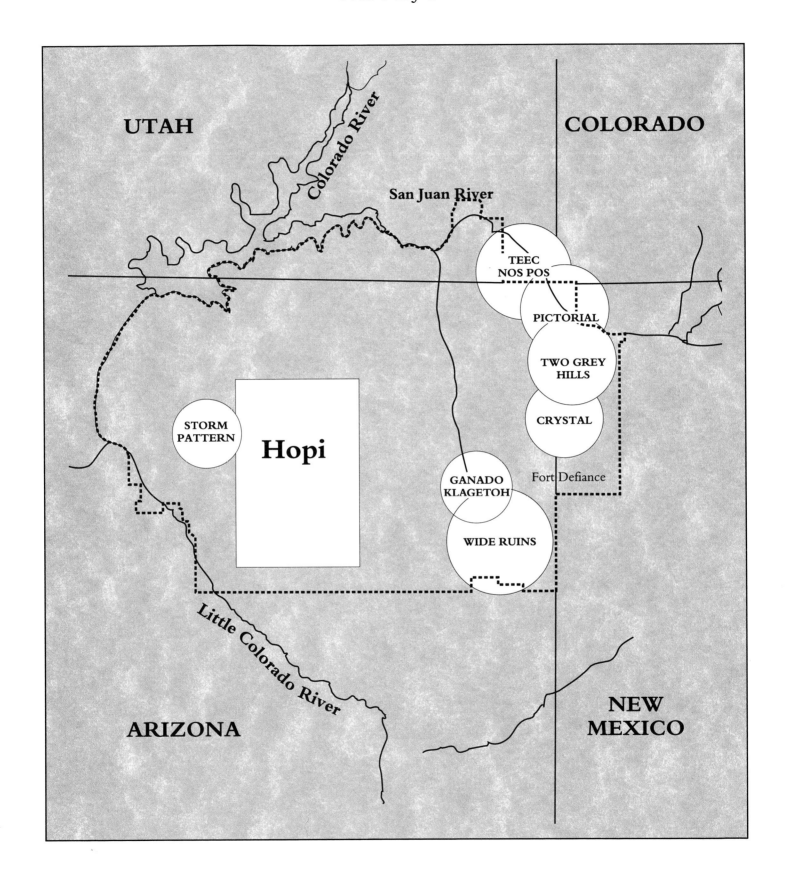

UTAH

COLORADO

Colorado River

San Juan River

TEEC NOS POS

PICTORIAL

TWO GREY HILLS

CRYSTAL

STORM PATTERN

Hopi

Fort Defiance

GANADO KLAGETOH

WIDE RUINS

Little Colorado River

ARIZONA

NEW MEXICO

modern Crystal style include many exceptional craftswomen, and the rugs are extremely smooth and finely woven. Their width is often greater in proportion to length than is common in other styles and the average size of the rugs is somewhat larger.

Weavers in the Wide Ruins area also make use of banded, unbordered designs in colors derived from vegetal dyes. These designs emphasize a range of soft pastel shades, recently moving from the traditional pale golds, greens, and tans into pinks, blues, and other shades. Synthetic dyes and blacks are virtually absent from these textiles. William and Sallie Lippincott, anthropologists who became traders at Wide Ruins in 1938, had worked with weavers to produce some exceptional rugs, and the style developed there is still characterized by very fine spinning and weaving. The wavy line pattern found in Crystal rugs is sometimes evident in Wide Ruins types, as are rows of a modernized version of the old serrated diamond pattern. The latter is sometimes called "squash blossoms." Wide Ruins rugs have a greater number of narrower bands and are generally more intricate in appearance than the Crystal style as well as being smaller in size and more narrow in width.

A number of variants of these banded, mostly vegetal-dyed types exist. Pine Springs and Nazlini, for example, also became centers for the production of natural dyed rugs. The Nazlini rugs

Working with her batten, this weaver slowly builds an elaborate design. The nubby appearance of the yarn suggests that it has been handspun, a rarity in modern Navajo weaving. The handspun warps and wefts will make for an extremely sturdy rug.

This Wide Ruins textile by Marie N. Begay shows the elaborate bands of squash blossom motifs and the compound stripes typical of the style.

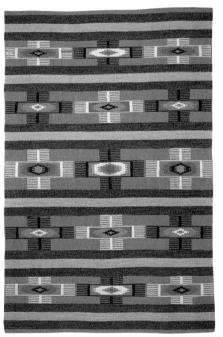

Ella Rose Perry wove this modern, unbordered Crystal rug. The Crystal area is known for the technological prowess of its weavers.

are distinguished by plant designs and a pinkish color made from crushed rock. Another type of rug with vegetal-dyed yarns comes from the area of Sawmill Trading Post. Large and soft, with medium and pastel tones, this style of rug uses larger, bolder versions of the old Chinle and modern Wide Ruins designs.

Despite the existence and popularity of these unbordered styles, the bordered rug layouts with their elongated central elements have remained prominent in Navajo weaving. Although they disappeared at Crystal, these style elements remained at Ganado and were combined with a deep, clear red to create the Ganado style. Modern Ganados are often very finely woven and feature two or more elaborate borders with a complex version of the central lozenge-shaped motif. Stepped designs rendered in black, gray, and white are included in the four corners of the

Blanche Hale weaves a fine Wide Ruins textile. Wide Ruins weavers often use the serrated diamond "squash blossom" as the primary design element.

bordered field. A similar type—often called a Klagetoh—exists in which gray outweighs red in the color scheme.

A highly prized type of modern Navajo textile is the style made in the vicinity of Two Grey Hills Trading Post. Like the modern Ganado style, it falls heir to the bordered central lozenge design of the J.B. Moore Crystal rugs. But, Two Grey Hills rugs are distinguished by the use of primarily undyed wools in tan, gray, brown, white, and black. Although the black is often overdyed with an aniline dye to deepen its color, the style is careful to maintain the natural tones of the wools of Navajo sheep. Borders are often double or sometimes multiple, and the lozenge and corner stepped designs can be quite elaborate. Navajo weavers generally are known for the density of their weaving, but Two Grey Hills artists are especially famous for the fineness of their spinning and weaving. They are often praised for their "tapestry" quality weaves, which may have weft counts as high as 115 yarns to the inch. Too fine to be floor rugs, these pieces are used as wall hangings.

The same style woven in reds in Ganado rugs and in natural wool colors in Two Grey Hills rugs is woven in vegetal and vegetal-color dyes in Burntwater textiles. The elaborate borders and elongated central lozenge are usually executed in pastel tones in the full range of colors of Wide Ruins and Crystal rugs.

Another area in which oriental rug design characteristics survived was near the Teec Nos Pos Trading Post in northern Arizona. Also a bordered design, the Teec Nos Pos features a variety of unusual, often geometric motifs that float against a neutral-colored background. Sometimes these designs are white, outlined in bright colors, or sometimes colored and outlined in white. The interior designs are not standardized, and the colors and yarns are usually commercial.

One of the most unusual patterns is associated with the western part of the reservation, where it is still woven today. The

This Teec Nos Pos textile by Cecilia George uses oriental design motifs, outlined in contrasting colors and floating against the background color. Bright colors are often incorporated into Teec Nos Pos textiles.

Though the classic Storm pattern was done in red, black, and gray on white, Lillie Touchin has woven this modern version in jewel colors.

Storm pattern is said to have Navajo meaning, but, more likely, this meaning was attributed to it by the enterprising trader J.B. Moore to enhance its salability. (If Moore did not concoct this meaning, then a weaver working for him may have.) In any case, the Storm pattern is characterized by a central box-like design (interpreted as a hogan, lake, or storm house), zigzag lines (lightning), squares at the four corners (houses of the wind or four sacred mountains), and figures said to be water bugs or piñon beetles. It is usually bordered and traditionally rendered in black, gray, white, and red. In contemporary versions, other colors may be also used.

The Yei, Yeibichai, and Sandpainting rugs do indeed contain figures that have religious significance to the Navajos. The

Yei rugs depict the Holy People of the Navajo religion. These Yei by Mary Yazzie are separated by corn plants. Note the elongated waists, which indicate holiness. The longer the waist, the more holy the personage.

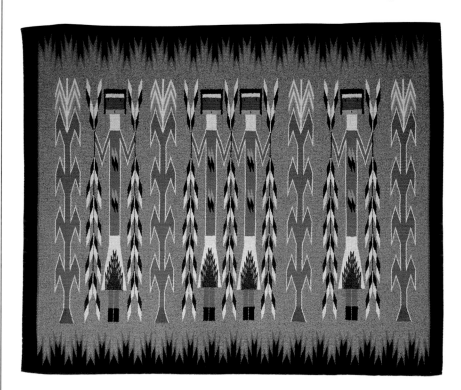

Lucy Nakai wove this rug featuring Yei-bi-chai, or Yei dancers. It won first prize in the 1978 Gallup Intertribal Ceremonial and second prize in the 1978 New Mexico State Fair.

rugs themselves are not used ceremonially and are made for sale like other Navajo rugs, but the Yei depicted are the Holy People, important supernaturals of Navajo religion. These stylized, humanoid figures are usually shown fully frontal with arms bent upward at the elbows. The Yeibichai style depicts a side view of a line of dancers costumed to represent the Yei, rather than the Yci themselves.

Much rarer are woven versions of the drypaintings used in Navajo curing ceremonies. These Sandpainting rugs are usually laid out to be looked at from any of the four sides, just as actual drypaintings are. Figures oriented to all four directions are depicted as part of the rugs' design, as are inanimate elements (rocks, mountains, or stars) that are integral to the story being illustrated. Although changes are sometimes made in the designs to remove the inherent supernatural power, many weavers still will not weave these types of rugs. Those who do have periodic ceremonies to alleviate any harm that may be done. Perhaps the most famous weaver of Sandpainting rugs was Hosteen Klah, a medicine man who considered himself both male and female. He practiced the female art of weaving along with the male ceremonial practice of curing, which included drypainting.

Stemming from late nineteenth-century attempts by Navajo weavers to record the images they saw in the world around them is a lively pictorial rug tradition that continues today. Early picto-

Vera Begay wove this Sandpainting rug called "Coyote Steals the Fire." Few weavers will weave representations of sandpaintings, which are not intended to be depicted in permanent media.

Pictorials may include any of a great variety of motifs. This pastoral scene is by Laura Nez, from a family of weavers known for their naturalistic representations.

rials include such expected imagery as cowboys, horses, and cattle. Modern versions of this tradition feature images that may seem surprising or unexpected at first glance but make sense given the original purpose of these pictorials. Today's rugs often contain steam shovels, pickup trucks, American flags, maps, hogans, mountains, dinosaurs, any variety of animal, and even Disney characters.

An interesting technique that gained popularity during the 1980s produced a style called Raised Outline. Usually woven with soft vegetal-dyed yarns, Raised Outline rugs are character-

This Raised Outline type rug, with a Teec Nos Pos design, uses a different weaving technology that leaves a low ridge of background color around design elements. This type of rug is common in the "new lands," which were added to the Navajo Reservation as a result of the Hopi-Navajo land dispute.

The Burntwater style combines vegetal shades with the design canons of the old Crystal and Two Grey Hills textiles. Brenda Spencer wove this fine Burntwater rug in 1986.

Wanda Anderson wove this intricate Burntwater textile, a style that combines the design forms of Two Grey Hills and Ganado with a palette of soft vegetal-type dyes.

ized by a ridge that outlines the design figures. This allows the pale background yarns greater prominence, softening further the contrast between the positive and negative forms in the design.

Along with many Burntwater and Wide Ruins rugs, Raised Outlines take advantage of a new group of specialists in Navajo weaving. These artisans specialize almost exclusively in the development of new dyes for yarn, primarily vegetal dyes. These dyes are purchased by other weavers who are then free to concentrate all of their time on weaving. This is an interesting step toward specialization in an art form in which women were traditionally involved in all phases of the weaving process.

The number of weavers has declined over the years, and the future of this art form with its stunning styles and intricate designs is undetermined. Bound up in tradition yet responsive to outside influences and markets, Navajo weaving remains a window that not only looks into the culture but out from it as well.

■ JEWELRY ■

The first Navajo to learn to work silver was probably a man called Atsidi Sani ("Old Smith"), who lived in the Crystal area. Some historians speculate that he learned the craft from a Mexican smith shortly after 1868, but there are indications that some silverwork was done earlier, specifically in the Navajo internment camp at Bosque Redondo. Atsidi Sani may have learned ironworking from the Mexican smith about 20 years earlier. At what point in the relationship the Mexican smith passed his knowledge of silverwork to Atsidi Sani is not known. Other experts suggest that more than one Mexican silversmith taught the craft to Atsidi Sani. It is best to assume that the start of Navajo silverworking occurred between 1850 and 1860 and may have developed from multiple sources. Before this time, the Navajos had made some jewelry from beaten brass or copper; but, with the adoption of silver, Navajo jewelry as it is known today began to develop.

Early pieces featured small designs that had been filed on, but sandcasting provided the means to conceptualize and then execute a whole piece. In sandcasting, the desired design is carved into two pieces of soft rock, which act as a mold when fitted together. Melted silver is poured into this rock. After the silver is removed, it is filed, polished, and finished. By the late

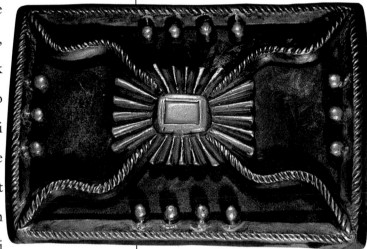

This sandcast bowguard, or ketoh, from about 1900 uses silver exclusively to form the design. The slightly curved X-shape is often associated with bowguards.

Navajo silversmiths either make their own die-stamps or buy them from another smith more skilled in that step of the art.

Turquoise is often used in Navajo silver to make the piece look and feel massive. This physical and visual heft is appropriate in a culture in which wealth and standing are illustrated via jewelry.

nineteenth century, the growing number of trading posts brought better tools to the Navajos, and they began to create dies for stamping designs into the metals, a technique that is still important in Navajo jewelry.

Until 1890, the chief source of silver for the Navajo smiths was American currency. Coins were melted or beaten to make jewelry. Sometimes they were mounted onto pieces intact. In 1890, the Currency Defacement Act prevented the Navajos from using American coinage in this way, so they turned to the softer Mexican silver coins as a source.

Another smith, Atsidi Chon, is credited with adding the other element so closely associated with Navajo jewelry. He may have been the first Navajo to set turquoise in silver, perhaps around 1878. Whether or not Atsidi Chon was literally the first has been lost in time, but this period does mark the beginning of the pairing of turquoise and silver in Navajo art.

By the turn of the century, traders were providing pre-cut and polished stones and sheet silver to the smiths. Thus, they were influencing jewelry making and encouraging it as a means of bringing Navajos into the cash economy. The traders also developed non-Indian markets for these and other Navajo arts.

Navajos, like their Zuni counterparts, now use a wide variety of stones and shells as settings in their jewelry. However, sil-

Contemporary Navajo jewelry has gone in many new directions, often using versions of inlay or silver overlay associated with Zuni or Hopi styles. These pieces by Vernon Begay show a combination of techniques executed with a distinctly Navajo feel for form and color.

ver remains extremely important as a visual element in itself. Stones are usually considered accents for the silverwork. Navajo smiths practice several techniques for decorating the silver, including stampwork, beading, engraving, and a technique that resembles filigree in its complexity. Silver designs of feathers and leaves often wreathe the stones. This elaboration of the silver usually indicates that a piece is of Navajo origin.

Navajo smiths use stones in a unique manner as well. They work with large nuggets more frequently than Pueblo silver-workers and are more likely to leave the stones rough in form. This combination of elaborately decorated silverwork and large, rough-cut stones results in a massive look to much of Navajo jewelry, in particular the older pieces. Also, years ago when trading posts acted as banks, silver jewelry was valued for its materials rather than its craft. The cash value of silver was determined by

Dating to the early 1900s, this bowguard demonstrates the strong central patterns so common in ketohs of this period.

Above: *This modern stamped and repoussé concho belt by Calvin Martinez, with its round primary elements, harkens back to the earliest Navajo belts.*

Above, right: *In this recent photo from Santa Fe's Indian Market, a Navajo woman combines a traditionally styled concho belt with a bracelet of contemporary design.*

weight, so the heavier the piece, the more value it held. Though in the twentieth century the Navajos have made jewelry for a non-Indian market that was interested in smaller, lighter pieces, the designs still reflect an aesthetic that prefers heft and weight in objects of value.

In addition to bracelets and rings, Navajos make a wide variety of jewelry. The beautiful concho, or concha, belts feature large or circular flat metal ornaments. They probably originated from the brass and German silver ornaments worn by Ute and Plains Indians. Navajos translated them into silver, and in time, they became the elaborate pieces found today. The celebrated squash blossom necklaces combine fine Navajo round silver beads with beads probably modeled on the flower of the pomegranate. Most characteristic of this necklace is its central crescent-

The beads in the turquoise necklace are
handmade from old coins, with a row of
pomegranate-shaped beads surrounding
the central najahe pendant. The other
necklace, is set with matched salmon-
colored coral and features a double row
of handmade silver beads.

shaped pendant, called the najahe. It was probably adopted from a Spanish-Mexican bridle decoration, which in turn derived from a Moorish charm to ward off the evil eye. Another distinctive Navajo jewelry type is the ketoh, or bowguard, usually mounted on leather and worn on a man's wrist.

In addition to the techniques associated with Navajo jewelry making, several Navajo smiths work in the overlay technique more commonly associated with Hopi and with the inlay and cluster/needlepoint styles developed at Zuni. The addition of stampwork to these techniques often designates a Navajo piece, as does the massiveness not usually seen in Pueblo jewelry or in Zuni inlay work. Despite any small differences, there are close parallels between Navajo and Pueblo silverwork, though the latter does not receive the attention of the former.

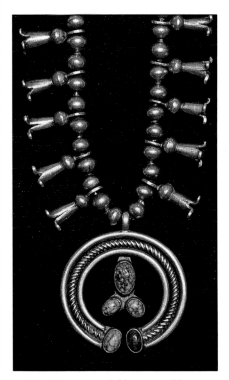

The older a squash blossom necklace, the simpler the design and the greater the emphasis on virtuosity in silverwork (rather than on the cut and match of stones). This example from 1920 illustrates this tendency.

This Gobernador Polychrome jar is from the period in which Pueblo pottery exacted its strongest influence on the Navajos. The Gobernador Canyon area is the Dinetah, the Navajo place of origin and also the area in which the Navajos and Pueblos lived as refugees following the 1680 revolt against the Spanish.

■ POTTERY ■

The origins of Navajo pottery are truly lost in history. Pottery may have originated as recently as the refugee period that followed the Pueblo Revolt of 1680. As such, it would have been part of the Pueblo influence that entered Navajo life during that period. However, pottery may go back much further in time to the thirteenth or fourteenth century, or even before. The same adaptiveness to new materials and techniques that makes Navajo art so exciting also makes it difficult to trace these arts archaeologically by the objects produced.

Navajo pottery as it is known after 1680 indicates influences not only from their Pueblo neighbors but also from the Plains Indians. The earliest type, called Dinetah after the Navajos' Southwestern homeland, was a thin-walled, coil-built grayware. Navajo utility pottery was wide-mouthed, bag-shaped, and characterized by pointy bottoms, which was typical of Woodland pottery made along the western edge of the Plains (Kansas-Nebraska). These characteristics also define very early Anasazi wares that predate it by a great deal, Apache wares, and some Eastern Pueblo wares, most notably from Taos and Picuris. The Taos and Picuris Pueblos also had contact with the Plains Indians. Navajo utility pottery was probably modeled after skin bags.

Another early eighteenth-century pottery style, Gobernador Polychrome, was a painted type that appears to have combined

Lucy Leupp McKelvey (Asdzaan Kiisaani) has pursued nontraditional directions in decoration and technology, but her pots "Buffalo People" (left) and "Cloud People of Windway" (right) use traditional Navajo religious themes.

features from several different Pueblo styles. After the mid-eighteenth century Navajo artists made less painted ware. They thickened the walls of their pottery and began to use an applied fillet decoration (always with a ceremonial break) that still survives in Navajo pottery.

Increased trade with the Euroamerican world and the availability of durable metal dishes and pots made pottery less and less useful to Navajos. Eventually, it was used primarily for religious ceremonies that required traditional pots. No tourist market developed for Navajo pottery in the early twentieth century. With the fall in demand, the number of active potters decreased. By the 1940s, the art of making pottery had become the part-time occupation of a small number of artists, and by the 1950s, it was produced almost entirely by the women of one clan in the Shonto area.

Navajo revival pottery is coated with pine pitch, giving it a red-brown, glossy appearance. Traditional Navajo pottery made use of appliquéd fillets of clay for ornamentation, and the revival pottery often features appliquéd forms such as the ear of corn on this jar.

One delightful aspect of the pottery revival is the creation of animal figurines. Sometimes they are free-standing as shown here, but often, as in the case of horned toads, they are attached to a pot.

Although Alice Cling uses traditional methods and materials, her work is carefully finished and contemporary in feel.

At this point, two traders at Shonto, Mildred Heflin and William T. Beaver, became interested in the potters and their work and purchased pots from them. Beaver began seeking outside markets, and a revival was born. This revival continues to be fueled by the current trader at Shonto and by Beaver at his Sacred Mountain Trading Post, as well as by other dealers.

Navajo pottery for the most part remains unpainted. Instead, it is covered with pine pitch and often enhanced by fortuitous fireclouding, which consists of discolored marks caused when pieces of burning fuel touch the pot during firing. As with weaving, Navajo pottery has shown immense innovation in the past forty years. It has also proven to be quite diverse; buyers can find anything from a simple version of a nineteenth-century form to a fat, knee-high fuzzy-bear bank. Pitched pottery tureens or punch bowls, animal figurines, and wedding vases covered with natural-looking, appliquéd horned toads may stand beside a bowl of zen elegance by premier potter Alice Cling. Pottery imitations of iron skillets and granite-ware coffeepots can be found, as well as eggshell-thin pieces of contemporary art pottery by Christine McHorse. It is indeed a lively art.

■ BASKETRY ■

As a nomadic people, vessels less prone to breakage became important to the Navajos. In that regard, baskets proved enormously useful. For example, the Navajos used basketry jars covered with pine pitch to hold water. Other types were used for gathering and preparing various foods, carrying burdens, and for other assorted tasks. Baskets were not only useful household items, they were also important parts of some ceremonies.

Baskets in Navajo life were considered sacred and therefore highly valued. At one time, it was not permitted to burn even a fragment of a basket. Worn and broken baskets had to be very carefully disposed of. Very fine ones were buried with the dead until the 1930s.

Navajo baskets were traditionally constructed using the coil technique, a slow and arduous process, and weavers had to

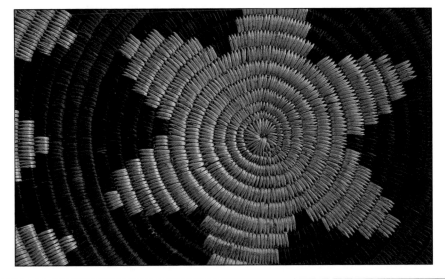

Mary Black, a Navajo-Paiute basket maker, has created a fairly traditional wedding basket. However, its outer design ring is one not usually found, and she has added to it a group of yellow-colored animals.

The coil construction of this wedding basket is easily visible. When these baskets are used to hold yucca suds for ritual washing, a piece of cloth is inserted in the center hole where the basket began.

observe a number of strict taboos in the making of baskets. (Coiling was not the only technique the Navajos used. They also crafted twine baskets that were similar to those made by the Anasazi descendants.) When basket makers of other tribes began to produce Navajo-style baskets, the Navajos, for the most part, were happy to trade for those pieces. Basket making by Navajo weavers declined steeply in the late nineteenth century. At the same time, the outside market for Navajo rugs was growing, and women turned their attention to that salable art form instead. Even today, many Navajo-style baskets are made by San Juan Paiutes.

The ceremonial, or wedding, basket is the best known of Navajo baskets. This basket style is recognized by its red band; bordering the outside of this band and included on the inside are rows of black, stepped triangles. The overall design has a break running through it, a "doorway" that is supposed to coincide on the outer rim with the place where the weave is finished off. During a wedding, this basket is filled with cornmeal mush, which is eaten by the bride and groom as well as the guests. Often, these baskets are sold following the ceremony, and they may be used and resold many times. When buying an old Navajo basket, it is not unusual to find remnants of cornmeal in its stitches.

The wedding design is the style most commonly seen today, but museum collections hold a variety of interesting designs from the nineteenth century. Spider Woman's crosses, as seen in

This fine basket by Evelyn Cly uses the colors and general organization of a ceremonial basket. She has also kept the center-to-rim "pathway," which points to the spot where the basket was finished.

Navajo textiles, were depicted on baskets as well, along with spirals, petaled stars, and complex terraced patterns. Black and deep red on natural backgrounds are the only colors found on these older baskets.

Today, different designs are produced by a new generation of revival basket makers who weave for the art market, at least in part. Some of these basket makers have returned to the old designs, while others have added new motifs, such as butterflies, cats, coyotes, and human figures. Recently, one particularly imaginative artist shaped a basket in the form of an octopus, with a traditional fret design forming the legs. Even Yei (Holy People) figures appear occasionally on baskets. Established designs are being altered: Wedding baskets, for example, are being produced with double and triple rows. The color palette has broadened considerably as well. Aniline dyes, with their full range of hues, are sometimes used as well as vegetal dyes, which have been discovered or rediscovered by contemporary basket weavers. Along with design and color, contemporary weavers have also manipulated the size of baskets. Extremely large baskets are produced as well as miniatures.

In the past 20 years, basketry has taken on some of the same innovative excitement associated with late nineteenth-century Navajo textiles and revival period pottery.

The use of butterflies in basketry design has recently become popular. The butterflies are often done in a variety of commercial dye colors, though this plaque by Grace Lehi uses natural dye colors. The flat, oval form is unusual in Navajo basketry.

■ SANDPAINTING ■

A sacred art, traditional sandpainting, which is also called drypainting, is employed to bring the Navajo world back into balance following some disturbance. This problem often manifests itself in a person's illness, and the ceremony cures by restoring harmony. The paintings are created by medicine men trickling colored sands and pigments through their fingers in precise patterns that tell religious stories. During the ceremony, the patient sits on the drypainting, which is then intentionally destroyed when its purpose is accomplished.

In this Edward S. Curtis photogravure, a religious practitioner creates a sandpainting by trickling colored sands through his hands in prescribed, precise designs. A sandpainting has curative properties and is important in restoring harmony. The loss of harmony causes illness.

Sandpaintings are beautiful as well as sacred, and non-Indian collectors have long been interested in obtaining permanent versions of them. However, it is not possible to possess a curing drypainting for the long term because their power is believed to be profound and potentially dangerous. As in the case of the Sandpainting rugs, pieces not made for ceremonies or slightly altered versions of the designs are considered by some makers to be powerless and therefore permissible. Choosing to depict only neutral or benevolent beings is also a way of protecting the artist.

Commercial sandpaintings, which use adhesive to hold the sands on plywood or particle board, have been produced since

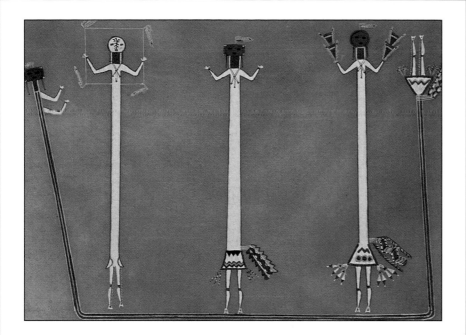

the early 1930s, when the craft was begun by a Euroamerican
couple for the curio market. The idea spread into the Navajo
community through a medicine man/artist. Commercial sandpaintings are often found around Shiprock and Two Grey Hills.

Another direction has recently been taken by artists who
paint sandpainting designs on muslin backgrounds. These suppos-
edly imitate "memory aids" made by medicine men to help them
with ceremonies. Matted and framed, these muslin paintings
allow the designs to be seen and enjoyed by outsiders.

The genius of the Navajos resides in their ability to take
technologies, motifs, and ideas from other societies and utilize
them effectively in their own culture—to turn outside influences
into something unique and distinctly Navajo. To come in contact with their art is to understand the Navajo history, culture,
and people—and to be richer for it.

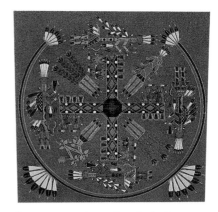

*Permanent versions of sandpaintings
(on boards) began to be sold in the
1930s. Traditional Navajos believe
that permanent sandpaintings should
not be done, or they should only be
done by someone knowledgeable enough
to control the power. This "Whirling
Logs" image is by Joe Ben, Jr.*

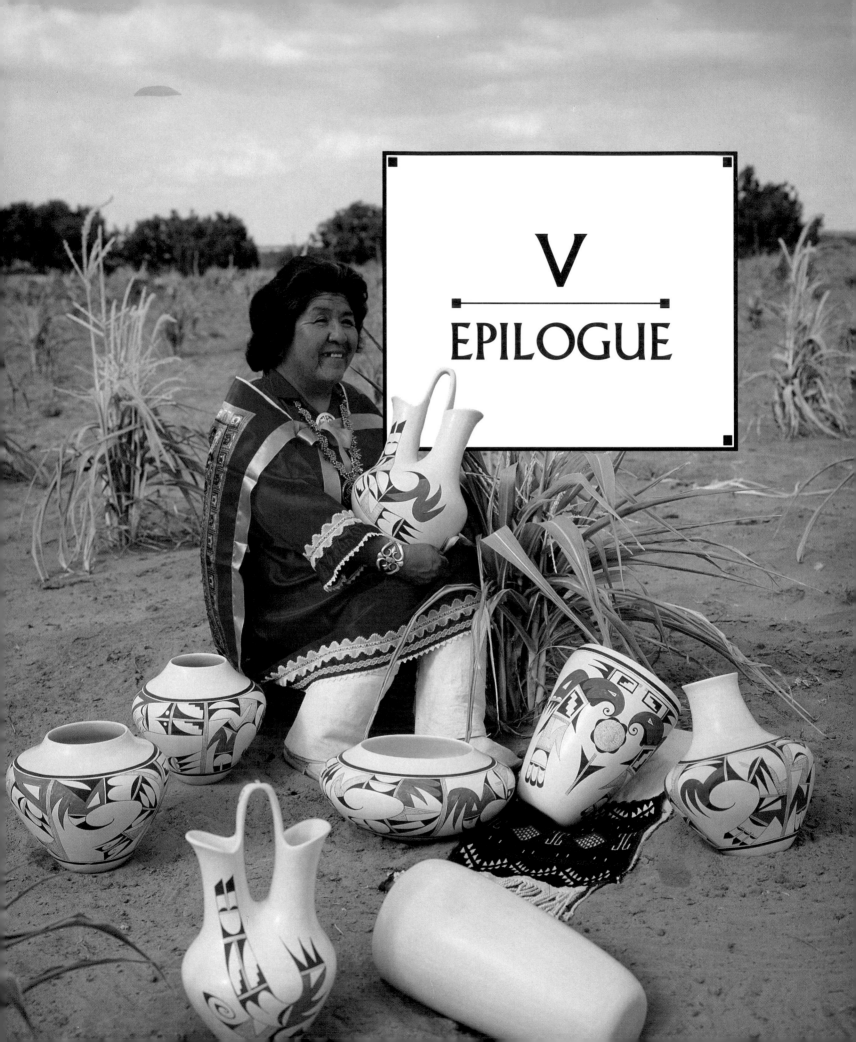

V
EPILOGUE

When Americans and Europeans began collecting examples of Native American art more than 100 years ago, it was with the idea that these pieces were curiosities. Early collectors thought these pieces and the people who made them were remnants of an era that was passing, absorbed into the unstoppable juggernaut of a larger, industrial society. But, a century later, most of these art forms are just as vital and dynamic. Contemporary Native American artists draw upon their traditions to translate new materials and ideas into vigorous commentary from a distinctly Indian perspective.

That is exactly the state of Southwestern Indian arts today. Most of the old arts survive within each culture; where an art form has been lost, arrangements have been made with other tribes to acquire examples of that art form through trade or other means. Thus, that art form is lost to one group but strengthened for another. And, new arts have been added—new media through which artists can express new ideas.

As the end of the twentieth century draws near, these old and new arts provide alternatives for Southwestern Native Americans, allowing artists to remain deeply centered within their cultures while facing the challenges of a new century with the means to make their voices heard and visions seen.

Opposite: *Joy Navasie sits among her beautifully crafted white pottery. She learned the art from her mother, Paqua, also known as Frogwoman. Navasie, who is Hopi-Tewa, has since taken the name Frogwoman. She carries on her mother's craft but has perfected the use of the white slip with red and black designs.*

GLOSSARY

Clusterwork

Coil-built pot

aniline—a commercially produced chemical dye sometimes used in textiles and basketry.

beading—in silversmithing, the use of dots of silver solder on a piece of jewelry as a decorative effect.

backstrap loom—a hand loom that is anchored at one end to a stationary object, such as a wall or tree, and at the other end by a strap passed around the weaver's waist.

carbon paint—in pottery decoration, pigments from an organic source, such as plant material, boiled to a thick paste and then dried in cakes.

channelwork—a form of inlay jewelry in which each piece of stone or shell is surrounded by a sliver of silver so that no two stones or shell pieces touch.

clusterwork—in silversmithing, the use of close groupings (clusters) of identical or similar stones to construct a design. Each stone is individually set in silver.

coil-built—in pottery, the manufacture of a pot by building up rolls of clay, which are then pinched together and smoothed on one or both sides to produce a continuous and unified surface; in basketry, the construction of a basket from bundles of fibers coiled around a center and sewn to itself.

dung-fired—in Pueblo pottery, traditional fuel used to fire pottery. Sheep dung is most commonly used.

effigy—a three-dimensional depiction of an animal or other natural figure.

fetish—a small carved figure, usually of an animal and usually carved in stone. Though traditionally possessed and valued for their supernatural powers, imitation fetishes are now also made for sale, primarily by the Zunis.

fillet decoration—the application of a decorative rope of clay on the outside of a pot. In Navajo pottery, it is usually just below the rim and contains a spirit break.

firecloud—a discolored mark on a piece of pottery caused by a piece of burning fuel touching the pot during firing.

Germantown—commercially spun, aniline-dyed yarns often used in Navajo weaving in the late nineteenth century. The name derives from the original town of manufacture, Germantown, Pennsylvania.

heart-line—in Zuni representations of animals, a line leading from the mouth to the torso of the animal. Found in pottery and fetishes, it represents the path of breath, which contains the animal's spiritual essence.

hogan—traditional one-room Navajo house. Hogans are round or six- or eight-sided and usually windowless, with the doorway facing east.

inlay—in silversmithing, the placing of stones or shell so that they touch each other without silver between them.

kachina—Pueblo ancestral figure who became a supernatural at death and brings rain and fertility to his people. The term can also be used to describe a dancer who impersonates a kachina in a ceremony.

kachina doll—carved representation of a kachina made within Pueblo societies to teach about the supernaturals. Kachina dolls are now carved for sale by the Hopis.

ketoh—Navajo term for bowguard, which is a guard to protect an archer's arm. The ketoh is usually made in silver and turquoise and mounted on a leather cuff.

manta—a wider-than-long rectangular textile worn over the shoulders as a cape.

medicine bundles— in Zuni fetish carving, containers for objects believed to contain supernatural power that are bound to the backs of fetish animals. Traditionally bound with animal gut or sinew, they sometimes contain prehistoric arrowheads or modern imitations.

micaceous—containing mica, a glistening mineral that adds a glittery look to the clay in which it is mixed.

mineral paint—in pottery decoration, pigments that are made from ground mineral ores such as hematite.

Kachina doll

Ketoh

Needlepoint

Polychrome pot

najahe—Navajo term for the crescent-shaped pendant on a squash blossom necklace. It probably derives from a Moorish charm used against the evil eye, which was used by the Spanish on horse bridles.

needlepoint—in silverwork, the use of small, individually set stones to construct a design. Versions using very tiny stones are called petitpoint.

overdyed—in weaving, the practice of dying to cover or intesify the natural color of the wool.

overlay—in silverwork, a technique associated with the Hopi that consists of a sheet of silver with a design cut out that is then laid over a second sheet of silver. The resulting cut out area is darkened to emphasize the design.

oxidized, or fired in an oxidizing atmosphere—in pottery, baked in such a way that all organic material burns out of the pottery, producing clearer colors away from the gray to black range. Iron ores in the clay will oxidize to a red color.

pitch—boiled pine sap, which is used on the exterior of Navajo pottery and water-bearing baskets.

plaiting—in basketry, a technique in which the wefts and warps are similarly flat and thin. Both elements are active, crossing over and under each other.

plumed serpent—a supernatural associated with water that is a serpent with bird-like characteristics, most notably feathers on the head or neck.

polychrome—in pottery, the use of three or more colors.

pound blanket—thickly spun, loosely woven Navajo blankets, usually simple in design, which were bought by traders according to weight.

reduced, or fired in a reducing atmosphere—the baking of pottery in an atmosphere sufficiently closed so that all organic materials do not burn out, and iron in the clay does not oxidize.

Saltillo—an eighteenth- and nineteenth-century weaving center of northern Mexico where Hispano-Moorish designs became well developed. Saltillo weavers trained Rio Grande Hispanic weavers early in the nineteenth century. Saltillo patterns heavily influenced Hispanic and native weaving traditions of the Southwest.

sandcast—cast in carved stone molds.

serape—poncho-shaped garment, often woven with a slit opening in the center of the textile for the head.

serrated diamond, squash blossom—a design frequently used in Navajo rugs that features a diamond- or lozenge-shaped form surrounded by a concentric sawtooth pattern.

sgraffito—in pottery, the practice of scratching a design onto a vessel after it has already been fired.

slip—finely ground, "liquid" clay, which is applied to the surface of an unfired pot. It can either be applied all over the surface to change the color of the body, or it can be applied as a "paint" to delineate designs.

Spider Woman's cross—equal-armed cross with small squares located at the ends of each corner. It symbolizes the supernatural Spider Woman, the patron of Navajo weavers.

spirit break, spirit line, spirit passage—an intentional break in a design for religious or ceremonial reasons.

storyteller—in pottery, a large adult figure usually depicted with its mouth open and eyes closed, with figures of children sitting on or near it.

temper—any non-plastic material added to clay to make it uniform in porosity as well as to reduce shrinkage in drying and to reduce firing damage. Sand, ground stone, or ground pot sherds are common tempers used in the Southwest.

warp—in weaving or basketry, the static elements that are extended lengthwise or vertically.

weft—in weaving or basketry, the active elements woven around the warp that are worked horizontally.

wicker—in basketry, the simplest form of twining, in which horizontal wefts are passed around vertical warps. In wicker, only one weft is used at a time, as opposed to the two that are used in regular twining.

Yei—Navajo supernaturals, or Holy People.

Yeibichai—a Navajo ceremony involving dancers costumed to impersonate the Yei.

Rug with Spider Woman's cross

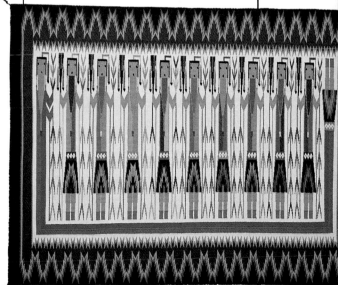

Rug with Yei figures

PHOTO CREDITS: